My Father and My Uncles

One Family's Call to Service

in World War II

Works by Jim Hodge:

Fiction

When Troubles Rain: A Novel

Nonfiction

***My Fathers and My Uncles:
One Family's Call to Service in World War II***

Short Stories

Every Man a Rifleman

Beer Contraband at 10,000 Feet

A Special Picture Remembered

My Father and My Uncles

One Family's Call to Service

in World War II

by

Jim Hodge

Red Recliner Books

an imprint of
DMS Onge Publishing, LLC
Hartland, Michigan
2025

Permissions:

Photo of Andrew Richard Dixon, Courtesy of Dixon Family Archives. Used with Permission. Photo of James McQueen Irvine II courtesy of Irvine Family Archives. Used with permission. Photo of Wilmouth Clark Hodge courtesy of Hodge Family Archives. Used with permission.   Photo of Donald Owen Morris courtesy of Morris Family Archives.   Used with permission.   Photo of Harry Hurley Hodge courtesy of Hodge Family Archives. Used with permission.   Photo of David C. Reed courtesy of Reed Family Archives. Used with permission.

Mucci's Rangers, by James McQueen Irvine, 1997 (previously unpublished). Used with permission.

WWII Mission Journal of Harry Hodge, by Harry Hurley Hodge, 1944 (previously unpublished). Used with permission.

Copyright © 2025 by Jim Hodge. All rights reserved.

No part of this book may be reproduced, scanned, or distributed in any printed or electronic form without written permission of the publisher.

My Father and My Uncles:
One Family's Call to Service in World War II
By Jim Hodge, 2025
ISBN: 978-1-944976-07-1 (First Hardcover Edition July 2025)
ISBN: 978-1-944976-16-3 (First Trade Edition November 2025)

First Printing
Printed in the United States of America

To the families of all those who served.

*Freedom is never
More than one generation away
from extinction.
We didn't pass it to our children
in the bloodstream.
It must be fought for, protected,
and handed on to them to do the same.*

Ronald Reagan

Contents

Preface 1

The Call to Service 3

Andy Dixon 7

Jim Irvine 23

Bill Hodge 51

Don Morris 65

Harry Hodge 79

Dave Reed 99

In the Passing Years 103

The Next Generation 109

Appendix A 113

Appendix B 207

Jim Hodge

Preface

Throughout my young life I had heard occasional remembrances about the service time of my father and my uncles during the Second World War.

A generation later, I entered the U.S. Army. In 1965 to 1966, I served in the 2nd Infantry Division at the hostile border between North and South Korea. I saw the determined effort of the then poor, but free, nation of South Korea, stand its guard against the aggressive communist dictatorship of North Korea–a dictatorship bent on the submission of the South to communist enslavement.

What I saw and experienced opened my eyes to the value of the contributions my relatives had made a generation earlier. The people of North Korea lived in subjugation and fear. Opposition to the ruling Kim family regime was met with imprisonment or, in some cases, execution. Abject poverty, including occasional starvation, was the norm.

It took many years before I finally began this project, but in 1998 I began to interview these aging men who had always been a part of my life. Their stories were something I wanted my family members to know about.

As I recorded their stories, I realized that this was something that could be shared beyond my own family. It is an American story. The story of how everyday Americans answered the call when their nation needed them.

J.H.

April 2025

Jim Hodge

The Call to Service

On December 7, 1941, the American naval fleet at Pearl Harbor, Hawaii, and the nearby Hickam and Wheeler airfields were attacked by war planes from the Empire of Japan. The next day, America declared war on Japan. Five days later, America also declared war on Japan's allies, Germany and Italy. All three of these nations had been waging war against certain other nations leading up to the Pearl Harbor attack. This war came to be called the Second World War, or World War II, soon after Germany attacked Poland in September of 1939. Now, with America in the war, it became an even more global conflict. The terrible war of 1914–1918 that had been known as The Great War or the World War, now became known as The First World War or World War I.

My Father and My Uncles

Six of my relatives entered the military service in World War II. They are four of my uncles, my father, and a man everyone considered a member of the family:

Andy Dixon, U. S. Army

Jim Irvine, U. S. Army

Bill Hodge, U. S. Marine Corps

Don Morris, U. S. Army Air Corps

Harry Hodge, U. S. Army Air Corps

Dave Reed, U. S. Army

Most of this story is about the journeys of these young men. Along the way, enough is mentioned about their civilian lives to indicate how they became related to each other.

For years I had heard bits and pieces about the wartime experiences of these men. It was not until I had them, and also their loved ones, supply me with a comprehensive picture of their experiences, that I was able to write this story.

Among the things that these five young men had in common as they grew up in the 1920s and 30s were these two things: they all came from modest financial upbringings, and none of them had really been anywhere.

They were soon to be spread out across the globe. Combined, they were on six of the earth's seven continents. Each man was a small cog in a large, sweeping piece of history, and yet, as I followed their accounts, I found a few coincidences that were a bit amazing.

Andrew Richard Dixon

Andy Dixon

Andrew Richard Dixon, the man who, soon after the war, would marry my father's sister, was the first of these men to enter the military service.

Andy was born in the southwestern Indiana city of Vincennes on April 30, 1917. The humble background mentioned earlier applied to no one better than Andy. At the age of twelve, his father passed away. Just a year later, his mother died. Andy and his older sister Hester were taken in by their Uncle Willie and Auntie Burt Fields. Andy and Hester's younger sister, Geneva, was taken in by someone else.

The Fields had a modest family farm, raising corn and rearing hogs and chickens, just outside the small community of Decker Chapel. This is in an area twenty miles due south of Vincennes close to where U.S. Highway 41, Indiana State Highway 241, and the White River all come together. Decker Chapel no longer appears on the Indiana state map.

The 1930s was a time of austerity and economic uncertainty in America. This was the time of the Great Depression. Employment was difficult to find. Home and bank foreclosures were common. As I look back on those in my family who were youngsters in the Depression, I am aware of that time's influence on them. Expendable income was a rare commodity. What money was spent was done judiciously. Over the many years of their lives, they conducted their affairs with responsibility and thankfulness.

Andy was expected to be a contributing worker on the farm. Despite having many responsibilities in a no-nonsense environment, he always spoke warmly of Uncle Willie and Auntie Burt.

In 1935, Andy graduated from Decker Chapel High School, where he had been a proud member of the basketball team. And this was something to be proud of. In those days, Indiana was considered the heart and soul of the American game of basketball.

After eight years on the farm, Andy, age 21 in 1938, did the same as many people at that time—he moved to the industrial north. Through his cousin, he secured work at the Sears and Roebuck store in downtown Pontiac, Michigan. In the spring of 1940, he was transferred to the Sears west side Detroit store at Oakman Boulevard and Grand River Avenue.

Andy needed a place to stay and he was soon directed to another Sears employee, Mrs. Claudie Hodge. Jim and Claudie Hodge—I would, one day, become one of their grandchildren—rented rooms at their home on nearby Cloverlawn Avenue. Andy took up residence there.

Throughout his life, Andy Dixon was able to make friends easily. His soft, down-home manner, humility, interest in others, and openness to share his own interests made others feel comfortable with him. Andy became like one of the family at the Hodge home. He took meals with the family, as was the practice of those who were not only roomers, but also boarders. I am specific about mentioning boarding because, for many years now, renting a room, and especially sharing the dinner table as a boarder, has long been a fading part of the American scene. Andy quickly became friends with the Hodge siblings: Bill, Harry and Hilda.

By this time, America, though still struggling, was slowly working its way out of the Depression. Andy must have considered himself doing quite well. He was assistant manager of the hardware department at the Sears store. But things were taking place in the world that would soon change the lives of many Americans. Our nation entered into war on December 7, 1941. It was then when the Empire of Japan, already at war in much of Asia, attacked the American naval fleet and air fields at Pearl Harbor, Hawaii.

For Andy, things began to change even before the Pearl Harbor attack.

In 1940, the year before the attack, the American government was concerned enough about the fighting in both Europe and Asia that it began to mobilize a number of National Guard units. Soon after, the government initiated the military draft. The draft required all young men beyond their nineteenth birthday to register for possible military conscription. Andy, who had a life-long love for hunting and fishing, was on a fall hunting trip in northern Michigan when he fulfilled his obligation to register for the draft. Shortly afterwards, in January of 1941, he received his induction notice.

Years ago, both my father and his sister told me that Andy believed that the small community where he registered found it most convenient to meet their draft quota by calling up a nonresident, instead of one of their own.

Thus, on February 13, 1941, nine months, three weeks and three days before the attack on Pearl Harbor, Andy Dixon entered the still peacetime American army.

Because the American government was optimistic that it would not have to commit to war, the draft commitment was for just one year. Song writer Mack Kay put the thought to music when he composed, "Goodbye Dear, I'll Be Back in a Year." The popular tune was recorded by a number of bands including Horace Heidt's group. With vocal by Ronnie Kemper and Donna Wood, the tune painted an optimistic picture of soldiers that would be returning to their civilian lives in a year. But for Andy and the others drafted before the attack on Pearl Harbor, things did not work out that way. It would be almost five years before Andy was mustered out of military service.

Andy did not have far to go for basic training. Fort Custer, just outside of Battle Creek, Michigan, had become a busy place in 1941.

Basic training took about eight weeks, but Andy remained at Custer until January of 1942, approximately eleven months after his arrival there. What he did during those months is unclear. One can surmise that he was assigned to duty in work that helped process the flow of trainees that were now coming through Fort Custer.

As 1941 moved along, the government was increasingly concerned about the situation in both Europe and Asia. At some point during that year, Andy and the others draftees with a one-year commitment were extended to eighteen months.

Andy received weekend passes with some frequency. He came back to Detroit on some of those weekends, hitching a ride with one of his fellow soldiers. On one such weekend in early December, Andy and his buddy were returning to Fort Custer on a Sunday afternoon. The date was December 7.

There is a five-hour time difference between Detroit, Michigan, and Pearl Harbor, Hawaii. From the time they left Cloverlawn Avenue, until the time they arrived at Fort Custer, word had come about the Pearl Harbor attack. One can imagine the feeling in the pit of Andy's stomach when he realized that his separation from the service after eighteen months was not going to happen. He was now into something much bigger!

Within a month's time, Andy found himself in Pomona, California, as a guard at one of several internment camps built to house Americans of Japanese descent. Here, men, woman and children, American citizens, were kept prisoner in a fenced-in, barracks-style camp. The American government, many years later, apologized for this action. The trauma of Pearl Harbor, and the perceived threat of a west coast invasion by the Japanese, overshadowed the fact that an American is an American, no matter his or her ancestry.

Andy remained as a camp guard at Pomona for ten months. On November 9, 1942, he was transferred to Camp Beale Air Base in the north central part of that same state of California, near the city of Marysville.

Here at Camp Beale, the Army was forming and training the 888th Ordinance H.M. (Heavy Machinery) Automotive Group. Andy was assigned to Company Q. On September 9, ten months after his arrival, his unit finally sailed for India.

Andy's unit sailed on the *Maripoza*. Judging by the fact that the ship did not have a military designation (i.e., "*U.S.S. Maripoza*") it must have been a privately owned ship that the government leased for use during the war. The volume of men and materiel to be moved about was so great that ships like the *Maripoza* were leased by, and put into service by, the government. Four of the six men in this account were, at one time or another, transported on such leased vessels. Sometimes these ships were mistakenly referred to as "liberty ships." Actually, "liberty ships" were government owned vessels that were built specifically for troop transport by industrialist Henry Kaiser.

It is unclear whether the *Maripoza* traveled alone or in a convoy. More than likely it traveled in convoy with other ships transporting elements of the 888th Ordinance H.M. Automotive Unit. It took thirty-three days to complete the trip across the Pacific Ocean and through the island-studded waters of Indonesia.

The *Maripoza* took dockage at the northeast Indian port city of Calcutta. Andy was now part of the China, Burma, India Theater, or the C.B.I. Theater. The war was so vast in nature that large pieces of the globe were given theater names as a quick way of recognition.

In 1937, the famous Burma Road had been completed. The road had been built so that China could supply itself through the back door, so-to-speak, in its war against the Japanese. This war between China and Japan had been going on since 1931. The difficult supply route had become a necessity for the Chinese because Japan had gained control of China's coastal ports.

Two hundred thousand Chinese laborers worked to construct the Burma Road from the Chinese city of Kunming to the Burmese village of Lashio.

Armaments and supplies for China entered Burma at the port of Rangoon in southernmost Burma.[1] The goods were shipped north by rail to the town of Lashio[2] in the mountainous east central part of the country. It was from here, at Lashio, that the supplies were trucked into China on the Burma Road. The road ran east across the border for seven hundred miles to the Chinese city of Kunming.[3] With its many switchbacks winding

---

[1] In today's world Burma is now known as Myanmar, and the city of Rangoon is now Yangon.
[2] One may find Lashio at 23° N, 98° E.
[3] Kunming is found at 25° N, 103° E.

through rugged mountainous terrain, it was a rare luxury to build the road in a straight line. Many lives were lost in its construction.

In April of 1942, the Japanese captured Lashio and shut down access to the Burma Road. By this time, Japan was not only fighting the Chinese, but all the allied nations in what had become World War II.

It should be noted that China, at this time, was not a communist nation. It was of interest to the United States, and all the free, allied nations of the world, that China stand strong against Japan.

Now, in order to get the materiel of war and other provisions into China, an Allied effort, led by the American 10th Air Force, began to fly "The Hump"—the towering mountains of the eastern Himalaya. From northern India across northern Burma into China this heroic, dangerous method of supply, was effective, but not nearly as efficient as the Burma Road. Lack of reliable charts, inadequate navigation aids, and the scarcity of accurate weather information made flying "The Hump" a costly campaign. A total of 594 aircraft were lost or missing and 1,659 souls perished or were missing in the effort. And yet, a vital 650,000 tons of goods arrived in Kunming thanks to this daring airlift.

By December of 1942, American and British engineers began construction of a road that began at Ledo,[4] a railhead town in the northern Indian state of Assam, near the Burmese border. This road, the Ledo Road, was to run 642 miles across Burma, in a rugged southeasterly direction, to the village of Mu-se.[5] Here, at the Burma-China border, the Ledo Road would run another 393 miles where it connected with the Burma Road near Kunming. If successful, the Ledo Road supply line would bypass the Japanese stranglehold at Lashio.

It was to the building of the Ledo Road that Andy's unit was headed. They arrived in Ledo that autumn of 1943, while the first and most difficult leg of construction was already underway. This was the 103 miles from Ledo to the Burmese village of Shingbwiyang. British engineers had surveyed this section in the nineteenth century, but any attempt at building a road had been abandoned. The closest thing to a

---

[4] One may find Ledo at 27° N, 96° E.
[5] Mu-se is found at 24° N, 98° E.

road were the foot paths made by Burmese refugees as they sought sanctuary in India from the aggression of the Japanese. The construction cut through the Pangsau Pass and wound through five ranges of the Patkai mountains. More than one hundred thousand cubic feet of earth per mile were moved in this section of construction. Steep grades and hairpin turns were a daily challenge.

In the monsoon season things became especially difficult. The new road gave way in a number of places. Because the newly cut road weakened the hillside above it, avalanches of mud and stone often came down on the road. In the heavy rains of May 1944, one battalion encountered one hundred avalanches in a thirty-two-mile stretch. Boulders as heavy as fifteen tons tumbled down onto the road. Dynamite was used on these large boulders before they could be pushed off the road. At times, trucks would bog down in the mud. Vehicles sank to the running boards. There was more than one occasion when a vehicle sank to its hood. Heavy equipment working farther up the road had to be called back to pull these vehicles out.

In front of the point of construction, American General Joe Stillwell led two Chinese divisions to clear any Japanese resistance.

Fighting could sometimes be heard by construction crews as they worked.

Andy's unit worked to keep the road builders supplied with the equipment they needed. He traveled part way, possibly most of the way, along the new road. There must have been times when repairing and replacing broken down equipment was done at a frantic pace.

After breaking through to Shingwibyang[6] the terrain became less severe in the Hukawng Valley.

Progress became swifter.

When construction reached the village of Mogaung[7] on the Namyin River, the thousands of Indian laborers on the project went home. They were replaced with thousands of Chinese laborers.

By late 1944, the Ledo Road reached the village of Mu-se. From there, the Ledo Road went on to connect with the Burma Road near Kunming.

On February 1, 1945, Nationalist Chinese President Chaing Kai-shek officially renamed the

---

[6] Shingwibyang is found at 27° N, 96° E
[7] Mogaung is found at 25° N, 97° E.

Ledo Road the Stillwell Road, in honor of General Stillwell.

On February 4, the first supply convoy of 113 vehicles reached the city of Kunming.

Fifteen thousand American soldiers took part in the Ledo Road project.

No doubt these soldiers felt a special sense of pride in what they had accomplished. By reopening the Burma Road supply-line the Chinese were more effective in fighting the Japanese. American lives were saved in the Pacific because Japanese troops in China could not now be transferred out of China.

Andy Dixon remained on the Ledo Road project until the end of the war. During this time Andy contracted a mild case of malaria and he was also bitten by a monkey.

On August 15, 1945, the Japanese Emperor announced that his nation would cease hostilities. On September 2, aboard the battleship *U.S.S. Missouri*, Japanese officials signed the unconditional surrender peace treaty.

On October 3, Andy Dixon left for the good old U.S.A. His ship arrived on the west coast on October 23. His orders then sent him to Camp

Grant, near Rockford, Illinois. He received $318.84 mustering out pay and his separation orders. Andy had been in "this man's Army" for four years, eight months and sixteen days.

~~~

Andy Dixon received the following medals, ribbons and citations for his service:

    American Defense Service Ribbon

    American Theater Ribbon, with one Bronze Medal Star and one Service Stripe

    Four Overseas Service Bars

    Good Conduct Medal

James McQueen Irvine II

Jim Hodge

Jim Irvine

Because Andy Dixon was drafted nine months and three weeks before the Japanese attack on the American naval fleet and airfields at Pearl Harbor, Hawaii, it was quite some time, eleven months and six days, before the next of these young men entered the service—James McQueen Irvine II.

Detroit has always been an east side, west side town. On the opposite side of the city from Jim and Claudie Hodge's west side home was the modest home of Jim and Elizabeth Irvine. The Irvine's had immigrated from Scotland in 1926 with five-year-old Jim and three-year-old Jenny. Just a year before bringing his family to America, Jim Irvine's boyhood friend, David Hunter, brought his family to America, settling in Des Moines, Iowa. The Irvines, in turn, went to Des Moines.

After only a year in Iowa, Jim Irvine brought his family to Detroit, Michigan. Jim hoped to, and did, get work with the Ford Motor Company. The Hunters came to Detroit a short time later.

The Irvines made the journey to Detroit in a Ford Model T. The car had no heat. Jenny remembers huddling under a quilt with her brother in the back seat.

Like many immigrant families the Irvines rented as they worked to get their feet on the ground. After eight years they were able get their own home on Cope Avenue on Detroit's east side. By this time two more daughters, Cathy and Elsie, had been born into the family.

Jim Irvine Senior, had fought on the battlefields of the Great War. My guess is that he could not have imagined that his son, wee Jim as he was called as a youngster, would also fight in another war that would encompass even more of the globe.

James McQueen Irvine II, grew into a determined and sincere youngster. These were qualities that he kept throughout his life. He was a good athlete. He competed on the track team at Detroit's Southeastern High School and he loved to play softball on the empty lots near the family home. On any playing field he was a fierce competitor. Off the field he returned to his mostly unflappable nature.

In 1941, Jim was twenty-one years old, working in the records file department at Vickers, Inc., an important supplier for the war effort during World War II, and he was taking a correspondence course in mechanical engineering. He was engaged to be married to Miss Margaret Gray. As happened to so many young men, his world changed abruptly after the Pearl Harbor attack.

Jim immediately tried to enlist in the Air Corps with the goal of becoming a fighter pilot. He was rejected because he did not pass the eye exam—strange since I don't recall him needing glasses until much later in his life. He then waited for the draft. He didn't have to wait long.

Jim Irvine was inducted into the Army on January 19, 1942, serial number 36 167 160. His place of induction was Fort Custer near Battle Creek, Michigan, the same place at which Andy Dixon, a man he had yet to meet, had been inducted the previous February. Records show that Andy had been shipped out to Pomona, California, roughly fourteen days before Jim's arrival.

Just months before his passing, in April of 1999, my Uncle Jim responded to my inquiry:

> *I was a little apprehensive about what might happen, how long I would be gone and very sad about leaving my family and my one and only. I did want to do my duty to rid the world of its oppressors and I did have a little anticipation of possible great adventure, which certainly did bear out.*
>
> *I was sent on a long train ride over hill and prairie to a far-off place that I had never heard of–Fort Riley, Kansas. I discovered shortly that it was the Cavalry Replacement Training Center.*

In the present year of 2025, it seems strange that as late as 1942 the American army would still maintain a horse cavalry. What one must remember, however, is that the Army had been neglected, undermanned, and under-equipped in the years between the world wars. The Army was still geared, to some degree, to use the horse cavalry. And so, Jim Irvine and his fellow recruits learned to care for and effectively use the Army horse.

My Uncle Jim's reply continued:

One of the great things about the assignment to the horse cavalry was that, in effect, I was instantly transported back in time to the days of the cowboys and Indians. Some of our sergeants were only two generations away from being trained by guys like General Custer. You could almost smell the leather and horse sweat and see the dust of the plains on their clothes. Some of them were like characters in a John Wayne movie. I never see a movie about the cavalry without identifying with the events and the men.

After basic training Jim was sent to Fort Bliss, Texas. This would now be sometime in April of 1942. Fort Bliss is near El Paso, close to the Mexican border at the Rio Grand River. This is the hot, dry, barren part of Texas known as "west of the Pecos" (Pecos River). I have been unable to find out what training Jim and the others received here but one can surmise that it involved advanced cavalry training or, in Jim's case, radio communication training. It was radio communications that was Jim's specialization while he was overseas.

Based on the extended time he spent at Fort Bliss—until early November—Jim was posted there well beyond any training time period. Despite the urgent need to stop the enemy's aggression, it was not unusual for troops to mark time at stateside military facilities, especially so early in the war. The Pentagon was scrambling to establish the logistics necessary to move massive amounts of men and materiel at the right time to the right place.

In October, Jim finally got a furlough. He came home to Detroit and it was at this time that he and Marge Gray were married. It was not unusual during the war for couples to go forth with their plans to marry, despite knowing that the man would likely be departing for another part of the world.

As my Aunt Marge related to me, they had a honeymoon of sorts that lasted almost three months. She returned with Jim to Fort Bliss, where she found off base housing. Jim lived in the barracks and they saw each other as often as possible. When, in early November, Jim was transferred to Camp Carson, Colorado, Marge again found off base housing for herself in the new location.

To understand the type of unit that Jim was transferred to we need to return to May of 1940, nineteen months before the Pearl Harbor attack. At that time the United States Army had formed the 98th Pack Mule Artillery at Fort Lewis, Washington. For the next fifteen months the 98th, with volunteers and an infusion of men from the draft program that had brought Andy Dixon into the service, built itself into a full-strength, well-trained unit.

The 98th Pack Mule Artillery was a battalion sized unit consisting of 760 men, one hundred horses and 695 mules. It was one of only four pack mule type units in the Army. As the name indicates it was an artillery unit that relied on mules rather than mechanized vehicles for mobility.

The Pack, as it was sometimes called, had the flexibility to penetrate areas where vehicles could not go. This would allow American artillery to traverse on foot paths and set up operations in otherwise inaccessible mountainous terrain.

It took six mules, with special saddles, to carry the parts for a single 105mm Howitzer artillery piece. Besides the artillery pieces, the mules carried everything else that the 98th needed: radio equipment, ammunition, grain and hay for the animals, food and water for the men, cooking equipment, tents, medical equipment for both men and animals—everything.

This was a rugged outfit requiring men with good stamina and a certain physical discipline about themselves. Many of these young men had been farm-boys from the Midwest or lumberjacks from the Pacific Northwest. Personnel in the pack artillery had to be a minimum of 5' 11" in height and weigh at least 175 pounds.

Included in the 98th's tough training while at Fort Lewis was a rugged 180 mile march on Mount Olympus in Washington's Olympic National Park with all animals, artillery and equipment. This training exercise was accomplished in April of 1942.

In August of that year, now nine months after America's entry into the war, the 98th Pack Mule Artillery was moved by train to Camp Carson, Colorado, to train at a higher altitude. The camp, for many years now, has been known as Fort Carson. It is just south of Colorado Springs on the Rocky Mountain's front range. To the northwest of Carson stands the massif of Pike's Peak.

That fall the men, mules, horses, artillery and equipment of the 98th marched the 14,000 feet to the top of Pike's Peak.

It was to this hardened, well-trained unit that Jim Irvine was transferred to just a few weeks after returning to Fort Bliss with his wife. The transfer took place sometime prior to Thanksgiving, 1942. Jim's name appears on the headquarters battery roster on Thanksgiving Day. It was with many of these men that Jim would spend the rest of his service time. He maintained contact with a number of them, including attending reunions.

Jim had only a few short weeks to familiarize himself with the men, the mules, the equipment and his job as radio operator for headquarters battery. On December 13, the 98th shipped out of Camp Carson by train: destination, Camp Patrick Henry, Virginia.

Marge took the bus back to Detroit. With the young couple tight on cash, she pawned her watch to pay for the bus fare. It would be two years, nine months and about two weeks before she would see her husband again.

The 98th arrived at Camp Henry on December 16. For ten days they marked time here, maintaining military discipline with constant inspections and close order drilling. Carbines and tommy guns were issued to the men.

The day after Christmas, the battalion boarded the *U.S.S. Thomas Jefferson* at the naval facility at Newport News, Virginia. The following day, destination unknown to the men, the ship began its journey down the Atlantic coast toward the Panama Canal. On January 2, 1943, the ship passed through the Canal. After a three-day layover at Balboa, the port city on the Pacific side of the Canal, the ship, now part of a convoy, began its trip across the ocean.

As is the Army way the men still did not know their destination. In a real sense the journey across the Pacific was a break for the men on the *Jefferson*. The horses and the mules were transported on another ship in the convoy–under the care of the men in the battalion's service battery. This relieved the men on the *Jefferson* from the constant challenge of caring for the animals. Just the thought of not having to clean up and dispose of manure for over six weeks on the Pacific Ocean must have created some thankful hearts.

On January 27, the *Jefferson* reached the island of New Caledonia. The ship held over briefly at the town of Noumea,[8] the island's major city at the extreme southeastern end of the island. From here the *Jefferson* traveled west-southwest to its Australian port destination of Brisbane. Arrival at Brisbane was on the first day of February.

The *Jefferson* had traveled through some dangerous waters on its way to Australia. Just a few months earlier, all the waters of the Melanesian Archipelago, even the coast of Australia itself, had been threatened with Japanese dominance. The enemy had been beaten back by the Americans in a great struggle on an island named Guadalcanal in the Solomon Island chain. As we will soon see in this story, it was another uncle who was one of those that prevailed on Guadalcanal.

After ten days in Brisbane, the battalion boarded a different ship—the *David Bushnell*. The ship traveled up the Coral Sea. It was not a pleasant journey for the men of the 98th. Most of them were quartered in the ship's forward hold. It

---

[8] Noumea is at 22° N, 167° E

was very hot with very little ventilation. The men slept on the steel plate decking.

On February 17, the men of the 98th Pack Mule Artillery arrived at Port Moresby, New Guinea. Port Moresby is on New Guinea's southern coast.[9] Jim Irvine and his fellow mule skinners, as they were called, had arrived to a world none of them had ever known. Tropical heat, humidity and rain were a constant.

Just to Port Moresby's north were the Owen Stanley Mountains. In July of 1942, seven months prior to the 98th's arrival, the Japanese had landed on the island's north shore, seventy-eight miles from Port Moresby. In August, they began to cross the mountains by hacking their way on the remote and difficult Kokoda Trail. From his headquarters in Port Moresby General Douglas MacArthur and his staff thought this an impossible task. Yet by mid-September, the Japanese were only thirty miles from Port Moresby. Here, Australian troops held off the exhausted, emaciated, disease ridden Japanese.

In the following weeks, Australian and American troops drove the Japanese back to the Island's north coast. Amid terrible coastal swamp

---

[9] Port Moresby is at 9° S, 147° E.

conditions and heavy losses, the allied troops defeated the Japanese here.

By the time the 98th arrived in New Guinea that February of 1943, most of the fighting was over. Only isolated pockets of resistance remained to be eliminated. Elements of the 98th were used for special assignments, but otherwise the battalion continued to patrol and provide security around Port Moresby. And, of course, they continued to train with their mules. As Jim put it in his correspondence to me, "We followed the wide butts of a thousand Army mules up and down the steaming foothills of the Owen Stanley Mountains."

As 1943 moved along, the once proud mule packers began to languish with the frustration of not contributing as they felt they should. Sixth Army Commander General Walter Krueger had yet to find a suitable combat mission for the battalion. By the end of the year, even training was lessened. Morale began to drop significantly.

In September, Jim Irvine and his buddy, Elmer Berg, had come up for a R&R (rest and relaxation) furlough to Sydney, Australia. While in Sydney Jim visited the USO, the United Service Organization

The USO was, and continues to be to this day, a place for service men to relax and enjoy a touch of home. It is customary for each service man to sign-in with his name and home address when entering the lobby. When Jim signed-in he saw that the name directly preceding his was Bill Harris, Anderdon Ave., Detroit, Michigan. Anderdon was the next street over from the Irvine home on Cope Avenue. Bill Harris had attended Jackson Junior High School and Southeastern High School with Jim. They were friends and had spent many hours on the softball diamonds in their neighborhood. Now, on the other side of the world, they had both entered the USO in Sydney, Australia, perhaps only a few minutes apart. Despite an anxious search, Jim was unable to find Bill Harris in the building.[10]

By early spring of 1944, General Krueger had made decisions that would put the 98th Pack Mule Artillery into the mainstream of the war in the Pacific. Sixth Army needed a tough, well-trained outfit to perform special missions for the

---

[10] These two men never did meet during their wartime service.

Allies' upcoming invasion of the Philippine Islands. In March, all the mules, all of the artillery, and some of the men of the 98th were sent to Major General Frank Dow Merrill in Burma. That regiment size outfit would soon become known as Merrill's Marauders.

At Port Moresby the 98th Pack Mule Artillery received a new commander—Lieutenant Colonel Henry Mucci.

As a youngster I can remember my Uncle Jim speaking of Colonel Mucci as a significant, probably the most significant, person in his military experience.

Mucci was brought in to retrain the mule packers into infantry soldiers. He was a 1936 graduate of West Point and a career soldier. Jim spoke of him as a dynamic leader that could, and did, do anything he ordered his men to do. Mucci was going to turn this already rugged outfit into one of the Army's elite Ranger battalions–the 6th Ranger Battalion. The significance of becoming Rangers and the leadership of Colonel Hank Mucci in making this happen can best be described in the tribute to Colonel Mucci written by Jim in honor of Mucci at the time of the

Colonel's death in 1997. My uncle's tribute is reproduced in Appendix B.

For the next three months, Mucci drove his men. They learned to do things in the valleys, on the mountain hillsides, and in and over the streams of their jungle environment that amazed themselves. The piece of land where they went through physical training became a quagmire of mud. They called it Misery Knoll.

In late July, the battalion left Port Moresby, the place that had been their home for seventeen months. Their destination was Finschhafen,[11] a settlement on New Guinea's north coast. Here they continued training into September. On September 25, the battalion was officially re-organized and named the 6th Ranger Infantry Battalion.

Fifteen days after their official recognition as Rangers, the battalion boarded three Navy destroyers. Their destination was north-northwest, to the Philippine archipelago. They were now going to be part of the massive effort to drive the Japanese from the Philippines.

---

[11] Finschhafen is at 7° S 147° E.

After steaming across the equator, the ships encountered a typhoon somewhere in the southern extreme of the Philippine Sea. The ships weathered the storm and it was seven days after leaving Finschhafen that they arrived at the place of their first combat mission as Rangers.

American forces planned to penetrate the Philippines at Leyte Island. Out in Leyte Gulf the Japanese occupied three islands: Dinagat, Suluan and Homohon. General MacArthur and Admiral Nimitz wanted the Japanese neutralized on these three islands to facilitate a smoother landing operation on Leyte.

The battalion, split into three elements, went ashore on the three islands on October 17, 1944. The missions were successful on each island. The 6th Rangers had helped pave the way for the invasion of Leyte Island by disrupting and destroying Japanese operations on the islands. The Rangers provided secure locations for signal lights to be mounted that would guide the two Leyte invasion Task Forces.

On October 20, U.S. forces made the landings on Leyte Island. It was here where one of the most famous newsreel pictures from the war was filmed when General MacArthur waded ashore, claiming that he had kept his promise and returned to liberate the Philippines. The 6th Ranger Battalion had done its part to make this possible.

An Army battalion is made up of a number of companies. In the 6th Ranger's case, there were seven companies: A through F, and Headquarters Company. As key operator radioman for Headquarters Company base radio, Jim Irvine was an important person in helping keep the entire battalion's communications successfully linked together. Headquarters Company includes the battalion commander and his staff, the battalion's medical officer and aid station, and certain equipment, including heavier weapons than the other companies have.

As base radio operator for Headquarters Company, Jim Irvine was Colonel Mucci's voice to his Company Commanders when face-to-face communication was not possible. Back then the equipment that Jim and the others in the communications section dealt with was not the digitized, hand-held equipment that we have today. The gear was bulky and heavy, requiring effort to transport and set up. Antennas, batteries, commo wire and a confident knowledge of Morse Code were the radioman's stock in trade.

Calibrating radios between company units could sometimes be tricky business. Lives depended on things being done right.

The Rangers stayed on the islands out in Leyte Gulf for almost a month, searching out and destroying the remaining enemy troops and guarding against any attempted reoccupation.

On November 14, the entire battalion was reunited on the big island of Leyte. They set up bivouac south of the town of Tacloban.[12] From here they began aggressive patrol action which continued until January 2, 1945.

By the coming of the new year, the Allies had the Japanese on the run throughout the archipelago. The Rangers were ordered to load ship on January 2 for the northern Philippine island of Luzon. This was the Lingayen Gulf[13] invasion. An advance element of the battalion went ashore on January 10. The rest of the battalion came ashore the following day. The battalion's overall mission here was to provide security for 6th Army Headquarters. In addition, elements of the battalion performed a number of

---

[12] Tacloban is at 12° N, 125°° E.
[13] Lingayen Gulf is at 17° N, 120° E.

specialized operations as the need arose. The battalion was, as my uncle described to me, 6th Army's utility player. These operations included reconnoitering patrols into areas where the enemy had a presence. On one of these operations a company of Rangers was sent 450 miles to the far north of Luzon. Here at Aparri[14] they captured the Japanese airfield.

Twenty-nine days after coming ashore at Lingayen Gulf, 6th Rangers accomplished a mission that made headlines back home. On the last night of January, they executed a raid on the Japanese prison camp one mile from the town of Cabanatuan. The Rangers rescued 486 American and 25 other Allied Prisoners of War (POWs). Many of these men had been captured three years earlier when the Bataan Peninsula fell to the Japanese. Regarding the rescue, General MacArthur reportedly said, "No incident in the Philippine campaign gave me greater satisfaction."

During the night of the raid Jim Irvine set-up and manned the battalion base radio in the bush near the POW camp. He stated that being a part of this rescue was the most gratifying mission

---

[14] Aparri is at 18°° N, 122° E.

of his military service. Jim and his fellow soldiers involved in this daring rescue would receive the Bronze Star.

Back home in the States, newspapers across the nation carried front page headlines about the rescue. In bold print the Detroit News headlines on February 2 read:

Prison Raid Frees 486 Bataan Heroes

Official List of   **All Jap Guards Are**

Saved Men   **Wiped Out**

The following April, *The Saturday Evening Post* carried Lieutenant Colonel Mucci's account of the mission.

Many years later, in 2005, Hollywood brought the story of this rescue to the motion picture screen in the movie titled, *The Great Raid*. Jim's role was not featured in the movie.

Just three weeks before his death in April of 1999, Jim Irvine received a letter of grateful thanks from one of the men who had been rescued that night. John Cook was hustled out of the prison that night wearing only boots and a pair of underpants. He had never lost his gratitude for what the Rangers did for him and the other prisoners. While he was alive, he attended a number of 6th Ranger reunions. For many years he either called or wrote to three different Rangers offering his personal thanks.

Throughout the rest of the winter and spring months of 1945, the Rangers distinguished themselves on a number of missions in helping to make the Japanese retreat to the far north of Luzon a costly one.

At the time of his 25th birthday in late May, Jim Irvine was given an assignment that he would never forget.

The Ranger's, at least Headquarters Company and most of the rest of the battalion, were operating out of the town of San Fernando, Pampanga Province, on the north shore of Lingayen Gulf. Irvine was given the task of delivering one base radio to an element of the Rangers that was operating out of Filipino guerilla headquarters in another San Fernando, this one in Elocosor Province. This was a two-hundred-mile trip to the north, through territory that was not entirely under Allied control.

Jim sped north with three other Rangers on what he was told would be a mission that would last for two days. In reality it was six weeks before he returned, alone, to Ranger headquarters. During this time, he spent most of his time behind Japanese lines, guided and hidden safely by the Filipino people of northern Luzon. He worked closely with a number of colorful and unforgettable characters, including an American Air Corps lieutenant named MacHenry. This man had become a guerilla fighter after the Japanese overran Clark Field three years earlier. MacHenry had been a thorn in the side of the Japanese forces ever since. He had become something of a god to the local people.

Jim also flew from an airfield that was just a small clearing on the side of a mountain. The small plane was piloted by a swashbuckling type of American pilot who was, at best, only half sober. He also saw how the Filipino locals dealt with a couple of their own people who had collaborated with the Japanese. At one point he joined a contingent of Filipino guerillas on a forced midnight march; staying just ahead of a pursuing Japanese patrol. On this escape they traveled through a mountain pass. Two days later, on a daylight return trip, Jim discovered how close he had come to falling to his death.

Near the end of his six weeks away from Ranger headquarters, Jim was quite a distance even from his original destination at San Fernando, Elocosor. Guided by locals, he traveled eleven hours on foot through the mountains to get back to battalion headquarters.

It was now summer, 1945. The victorious Luzon campaign came to a close.

Almost all the mighty gains made by the Japanese Imperial Army and Navy throughout Asia and the Pacific had been reclaimed by the Allies. In Europe, the war against Germany had ended in May. The only obstacle remaining to overcome for the world to return to peace was a big one—the defeat of the Japanese home islands. The Japanese refusal to surrender meant that the invasion of the home islands would require a cost in human life that would make anything else in the war pale by comparison. Jim Irvine and his fellow Rangers knew it would be a long time before they would return home to build their lives.

And then, on August 6, the world changed forever. By order of President Harry Truman, a new weapon, the atomic bomb, was dropped on the Japanese city of Hiroshima. Despite the utter devastation, the Japanese refused to surrender. In less than a week, a second atomic bomb was dropped on the city of Nagasaki. Japan sued for peace. The Second World War was over.

Within a few days, Jim and the other veterans who had acquired enough points, went home. The 6th Ranger Battalion continued to distinguish itself as part of the Army of Occupation at Kyoto, Japan, until it was demobilized on December 30, 1945.

On September 21, 1945, Jim's ship arrived in San Francisco Bay. His orders had him to report to Fort Sheridan, Illinois, on October 5 for separation. The days between his arrival in San Francisco and his report date at Fort Sheridan were his to do with as he saw fit. He came home to Detroit, and his arrival home was attended by unusual circumstances.

September 27, 1945, was an exciting day at the Irvine home on Cope Avenue.

That morning, Jim Irvine's sister Jenny welcomed the arrival of her husband, Harry Hodge. Harry had just been separated from military service at Westover Air Field in Massachusetts. His story is one we will look at shortly. Harry's arrival was expected and after he arrived at mid-morning Jenny knew that they were now beginning their lives together.

That same day, a few hours later, Jim Irvine arrived in Detroit. He had not informed his family of his whereabouts. They thought he was still overseas. He went first and surprised Marge, who was living with her parents on Dickerson Avenue. The young couple that had been married for three years, but had spent only the first three months together, were reunited.

Still in uniform, Jim walked the three blocks over to Cope Avenue and knocked on the front door. Jenny went to the door to answer it. Of course, her feet had not touched the ground all day since Harry's arrival. She opened the door to see her brother, who was totally unexpected. She simply sank to the floor in the doorway and sobbed, overcome with the emotion of this great day.

Jim Irvine was back home after three years, eight months, and eleven days.

~~~

Jim Irvine received the following medals, ribbons and citations for his service:

    Bronze Star

    Combat Infantryman's Badge

    Philippine Liberation Medal

    Philippine Liberation Ribbon

    Good Conduct Medal

    Asiatic Pacific Campaign Ribbon

    Efficiency Fidelity Honor Medal

My Father and My Uncles

Wilmouth Clark "Bill" Hodge

Jim Hodge

Bill Hodge

While Andy Dixon was driving back to Fort Custer on December 7, the day of the Pearl Harbor attack, my father's brother was at the family home on Cloverlawn Avenue. He was eating dinner with his parents when word of the attack reached the Hodge home.

Wilmouth Clark Hodge, Bill as we called him, was born in Lynnville, Tennessee, on January 24, 1920. He, his younger brother Harry, and their infant sister Francis Hilda, moved to Detroit, Michigan with their parents, Jim and Claudie Hodge, in 1925.

The family rented at several places for eleven years until buying the foreclosed home on Cloverlawn Avenue in 1936. The large home included three bedrooms upstairs that Claudie

Hodge rented out. It was to this room and board situation that Andy Dixon had arrived in 1940.

In 1931, at age eleven, Bill and his little brother Harry, age nine, went back to Lynnville to spend part of the summer on the farm of their Uncle John Clark. Except for this, and one later trip to Lynnville, Bill and Harry's world did not extend beyond the Detroit area.

Soon after the attack at Pearl Harbor, Bill volunteered for the Marine Corps. He entered the service on February 9, 1942, serial number 036440. Boot camp was at Parris Island, South Carolina.

Corresponding by mail he described to me:

I was twenty-two years old at the time. After boot camp I was stationed at Parris Island for about a month and then transferred to New River, North Carolina, where they were forming the 1st Marine Division. I was assigned to the 11th Regimental Artillery and spent about two months training there. We then traveled by train to San Francisco and shipped out for Wellington, New Zealand, for further training.

Bill's regiment shipped out for New Zealand on what had been a luxury Swedish liner, the *Ro Sham Bo*, in the latter part of June.

When August began, the 1st Division, minus the 7th Regiment—they would rejoin the Division on September 18—shipped out of Wellington for the island of Fiji. Here they went through amphibious assault maneuvers.

The proficiency of the maneuvers was considered unimpressive by the Navy brass and by General Alexander Vandegrift, commander of the 1st Marine Division. Nonetheless, the Division was ordered to assault Guadalcanal Island on August 7.

It was a month previous to this time when Naval intelligence at Pearl Harbor had learned, through its ability to break the Japanese code, that the Japanese were hurriedly constructing an airfield on the island of Guadalcanal. Once completed, the airfield would allow the Japanese to make a renewed bid for air superiority over the Coral Sea and also close the sea approaches to eastern Australia. For these reasons control of this obscure though goodly sized island in the South Pacific became vital.

My Father and My Uncles

The taking of Guadalcanal[15] was code named Operation Watchtower. Bill and his fellow Marines were not briefed on where they were headed until shortly before the amphibious landing. They had hoped the target was a palm fringed paradise. They were about to be disappointed.

Guadalcanal lies along the same humidity drenched latitude as Port Moresby. Because it has a mountainous spine 8,000 feet high, the island is shrouded in clouds and receives heavy rainfall all year long. The jungle canopy is dense. Little sunlight penetrates to the jungle floor. All this moisture creates a fermented rot of vegetation which gives off a sickening stench.

It is beyond the scope of this story to give a running account of all that happened on this island in the four months that Bill Hodge was there, but an understanding of the overall picture and a small amount of what he experienced follows.

At midnight, August 6, the ships carrying the 1st Marine Division approached the area offshore from the partially completed airfield. The comparatively small force of Japanese was caught

---

[15] Guadalcanal is in the Solomon Island chain due east of New Guinea at 9° S, 160° E.

completely by surprise. The Marines received some resistance but most of the enemy escaped into the jungle.

The nightmare of Guadalcanal was not the taking of the airfield, but rather holding on to it. The Japanese quickly began to build up troop strength on the island. Within less than two days after the Marines arrived on the island, the U.S. Navy suffered its most one-sided defeat ever. Under the cover of darkness Japanese warships surprised our Navy in the offshore water that became known as Iron Bottom Sound. Three American cruisers and an Australian cruiser were sunk.

For the next three-and-a-half months the fight for control of the airfield was a vicious land, sea, and air battle. At their dug-in perimeter around the airfield the Marines learned how fanatical the Japanese soldier was. The Marines fought off a number of frontal charges. The attacks came at night and there were a number of cases of hand-to-hand fighting. The two sides were so close to each other that, when all else was quiet, the Marines could hear the Japanese talking to themselves. Sometimes the Japanese taunted the Americans. Names like the Battle of the Tenaru River, the Battle of Edson Ridge, the

Battle of Bloody Ridge, and others became nights that would disturb many of these Marines for a long time.

During the daylight hours the Marines ran constant patrols to try and keep the enemy off balance.

Bill was assigned to the motor pool and he was personal driver to General P.A. Davalle. As Bill wrote to me:

> General Devalle was regimental commander of the 11th Artillery Regiment. It was my responsibility to keep the General alive at all times. The General was the best artillery man I ever saw.

On the night the three American cruisers and one Australian cruiser were sunk, Bill was manning a fifty-caliber machine gun. It was only the second day that the Marines were on the island. Bill and his crew hastily mounted the gun into position in the dark. When morning came Bill and those with him saw that they had mounted the gun in the middle of a gasoline dump of fifty-five-gallon drums. One hit on the dump and they all would have been blown sky high. Providence was with them.

My father, Bill's brother, was following his brother's ordeal on Guadalcanal as best he could. I found in my father's box of keepsakes from the war an old faded, curled up article he cut out from *The Detroit News*. The article is dated September 16, 1942. It is by United Press staff correspondent Robert Miller. The article describes much of what went on during the two nights of September 12 and 13. It reveals how much was required of the Marines to prevent themselves from being overrun. Some breaches in the perimeter occurred only to be shored up with fighting at such close quarters that the rifle bayonet was the final weapon of defense.

Bill recalled those two nights. They became known as the Battle of Edson Ridge:

> *We were firing our 105's [105 Howitzer artillery guns] with an elevation so that the shell was going almost straight up and coming down on the face of the hill that the Japs were trying to get up.*
>
> *I had a fifty-caliber machine gun set up at the foot of Edson Ridge. Every now and then the Japs would shout, 'Marines, you die'. You can guess what we shouted back. That was the night that Colonel Edson*

received the Congressional Medal of Honor.

As the weeks went by on Guadalcanal, Bill participated in a number of patrols that went out daily from the perimeter. In following up his written responses to my questions he told me over the phone of one incident. He was point-man on a patrol when a Japanese soldier jumped out from behind a tree and fired at him from point blank range. The rifle misfired. Bill was carrying a Thompson submachine gun. He took out the Japanese soldier.

Bill said the worst thing he ever lived through was the night the two Japanese battleships shelled the airfield and much of the surrounding perimeter. This was the night of October 12. The battleships *Kongo* and *Haruna* had entered Iron Bottom Sound during the night. At midnight they began lobbing shells from ten miles out. These battleships had the capacity to fire huge fourteen-inch shells.

Out of ninety planes at the airfield only eleven were operational after the shelling. The steel matting on the airfield runway was shredded like cardboard. Forty-one Marines and soldiers of the newly arrived Army's Americal Division were killed that night. Bill came very close to being one of those killed, as he described to me:

> *The shells were coming in three at a time. They sounded like a freight train locomotive.*
>
> *I was in a coral reinforced dugout with sixteen other Marines when one Jap shell went through three and a half feet of coral and exploded in the dugout. Myself and two other Marines were blown out of the opening of the dugout. The other thirteen Marines were killed. They were covered over by a bulldozer. Buried right there where they died.*

One of Bill's eardrums was blown out from the shell's concussion. Eventually, the Veteran's Administration rated his right ear as "profound hearing loss" and his left ear as "serious to profound loss."

The fierce naval battles of November 13, 14 and 15 finally broke the will of the Japanese to take back the airfield. The 1st Marine Division was relieved in early December. Bill left the island on December 9, 1942.

Be it known that the struggle and sacrifice of the 1st Marine Division, the Americal Division,

Marine and Air Corps pilots, and the Navy at this bloody place were truly important. Many lives were saved later because these servicemen held their ground at Guadalcanal.

From the island, Bill and his fellow Marines shipped down to Brisbane, Australia. This was about a month before Jim Irvine's layover there. The Marines did not stay there long. It was discovered that Brisbane was home to the malaria carrying female anopheles mosquito. The division went further south to Melbourne where the climate was cooler. Bill's 11th Regiment was soon sent to Ballarat, a midsize town to the northwest of Melbourne. Here the regiment spent time recuperating from their ordeal on Guadalcanal. A goodly percentage of the men, including Bill, were suffering from malaria. He would have recurrences of this disease for the next five years. Some men had infections from the jungle environment. Compounding his hearing loss, Bill suffered from the ear infection that the men knew simply as "jungle rot."

In the fall of 1943 General Devalle and his driver, Bill Hodge, were recalled to Marine Headquarters at Quantico, Virginia. Amazingly, they shipped home on the *Ro Sham Bo*—the same vessel that had brought them to the South Pacific.

From Melbourne, the route home was supposed to take the *Ro Sham Bo* between the North and South Islands of New Zealand. However, strong Japanese submarine activity was reported in the area so the *Ro Sham Bo* skirted below the South Island instead. This is an area of the Tasman Sea known for fierce storms. The ship encountered a terrible storm. In the bowels of the vessel Bill anchored himself to a stanchion with his web belt. Had he not done this he would have been slammed back and forth with each roll of the ship. Secured to the stanchion was an instrument which registered the ship's list. The *Ro Sham Bo* was built to handle a list of up to 28 degrees. Bill saw the instrument register a list of 33 degrees. After the storm Bill went topside. Everything that had not been fastened down had either slid overboard or was smashed to pieces.

While at Quantico, General Devalle went to bat for Bill. He got Bill enrolled into Reserve Officer Candidate School. Bill graduated from this rigorous program on March 22, 1944. His new serial number was 367277. His remaining time as an enlisted man was canceled and replaced by his reserve officer commission. He now officially served at the discretion of the government. Of course, in reality, that was his status during war time as an enlisted man. If the war had continued after his four-year enlistment had run-out he would have been retained for the duration of the war, enlisted man or officer.

During his time at Quantico, Bill met Gloria Paige. She was from Eagle River, Wisconsin, serving in the Marine Corps as a W.M., or Woman Marine. Bill and Gloria married while at Quantico.

After receiving his commission Bill, now a 2nd Lieutenant, was transferred to the big Marine base at Camp Pendleton, Oceanside, California. Here he took administrative duties at the Officer Replacement Draft.

It was at this time that Bill had another bout with malaria. After his recovery his assignment was changed. He remained at Pendleton but was now assigned to the Troop Leaders School, where noncommissioned officers received leadership training. Bill stayed here for the remaining months of the war. It was while here that he was promoted to 1st Lieutenant.

Bill Hodge had survived one of the most savage campaigns of the war; the battle for Guadalcanal Island. He had then gone on to receive his officer's commission.

My uncle told me he wouldn't trade his experience as a Marine for a million dollars, but that he would not do it again for all the money in the world.

Bill Hodge was separated from active duty on December 3, 1945. He remained in the Marine Corps Reserve until January of 1952.

~~~

Bill Hodge received the following medals, ribbons and citations for his service:

    Good Conduct Medal

    American Campaign Ribbon

    Asiatic Pacific Combat Action Ribbon for engaging the enemy on an amphibious assault on Guadalcanal

    Navy Presidential Ribbon

    WW II Victory Medal

Donald Owen Morris

Jim Hodge

Don Morris

Our story now takes us back, once again, to Detroit's east side.

Donald Owen Morris was born on November 20, 1925, in the home his parents were renting on McCellan Avenue. Like the other young men in this story, his was a modest upbringing. The Morris's struggled through the Depression like so many other people did. At one place where they rented, they lived in a garage near a lake. Don remembers his mother walking down to the lake with a bucket to get water for washing.

In 1935 the Morris's moved to 4126 Gray Avenue. Don was sixteen years old when the United States entered the war in December of 1941.

When he turned seventeen in November of 1942, Don tested for, and was accepted into, the Air Corps Cadet Program. This was a program which allowed high school seniors to take introductory classes related to the Air Corps while finishing the last year of high school. The plan was that this would be a starting point for young men to eventually become officers after they entered the Air Corps.

Don finished high school that winter and he immediately enlisted in the Air Corps. He was inducted on January 7, 1943. He was shipped off to Keasler Field in Biloxi, Mississippi, for basic training. The Air Corps at this time was still a part of the Army. It was not until two years after the war that the Air Corps became the Air Force; a separate part of the Department of Defense.

After basic training, the cadet program that Don started in high school allowed him to be sent to Carbondale University in Carbondale, Illinois. Here, he and other cadets continued in the program. This was school with rigid discipline. College classes were taught with emphasis on math and science. Subjects related specifically to the Air Corps, such as navigation, were taught. The part of the cadet program carried out at

Carbondale was considered pre-flight training by the Air Corps.

In September of that year, the Air Corps suddenly cut back on the cadet program. They eliminated everything from pre-flight back. Any hope Don had of gaining an officer commission was dashed.

Everyone at Carbondale was reassigned. Those with initials A through K were sent to Fort Leonard Wood, in Missouri for infantry training. Don Morris stayed in the Air Corps. He was sent to Las Vegas, Nevada, for air gunnery school.

Training at air gunnery school put heavy emphasis on learning to lead a target when both the target and the shooter were moving. Don and his fellow trainees shot a twelve-gauge shot gun from the bed of a moving quarter ton pickup truck at moving clay pigeons. They progressed to firing the thirty-caliber machine gun at a moving target from the bed of a moving two-and-half ton truck. They then learned to fire the thirty-caliber from the open cockpit of a plane in flight. These planes were similar to, but more advanced than, those flown in World War I. The target was a large paper or light weight cloth pulled behind another plane.

Though these exercises lacked realism, I have been told by Don Morris and Harry Hodge, the next man in this story, that the training was effective. The ability to accurately lead a moving target, while moving yourself, was learned.

After gunnery school, Don was sent to radio school in Sioux Falls, South Dakota. He was then sent to Lincoln, Nebraska. This was one of the locations where the Air Corps formed the ten-man crews for the B-17 bomber. Here, Don was put on a crew that would train as a unit, fly overseas as a unit and, if all went well, fly many bombing missions as a unit. The plane these men trained on in Lincoln was the plane they would take overseas. While there at Lincoln, Don crossed paths with his best friend, Jack Gray. Jack had been assigned to the Air Corps. He was in Lincoln for crew assignment as well.

Don's crew flew to Ardmore, Oklahoma, for further training. The thirty-caliber machine gun they had trained with earlier was replaced with the bigger, more powerful fifty-caliber.

The B-17 was known as the "Flying Fortress." This plane was the workhorse heavy bomber of the American Army Air Corps. Like all aircraft at that time, it was propeller driven. The

Air Corps employed other heavy bombers during the war—most notably the B-24, the B-25, and the B-26. None of them could match the B-17 for durability, maneuverability, and penetration at high altitudes.

With training completed at Ardmore, Don and his crew mates were ready for overseas duty. They were given orders for Britain. They would be joining the 8th Air Force.[16] Each Air Force consisted of a number of bomber Wings. A bomber Wing consisted of six Groups. Each Group consisted of four Squadrons and each Squadron consisted of, at full strength, nine planes—each plane with a ten-man crew.

From Ardmore, Oklahoma, Don's plane, piloted by Eldred Schumaker, flew to New York where it landed for refueling. From New York the plane flew to the Canadian airfield at Goose Bay, Labrador.[17] This was the jumping off point for a flight across the Atlantic, via Iceland. Goose Bay was an austere place. But it was an important place. By refueling at Goose Bay, the B-17 had enough fuel to make it to Iceland.

---

[16] It should be noted that when referring to the 8th or any other numbered Air Force unit that these were units within the larger Army Air Corps.
[17] Goose Bay is at 54° N, 60° W.

Don recalls that they spent about eight hours on the ground in Iceland. The airfield was leveled out of an area surrounded by a barren, red lava landscape. He tried fitfully to sleep.

From Iceland the plane flew on to the airfield in England to which it had been ordered to land. The plane and crew were assigned to the 8th Air Force's 452nd Bomb Group, 728th Squadron. Their airfield was Deophan Green, Attleborough, England.[18]

It was now winter, 1944. The 8th Air Force's assignment had been, and continued to be, to conduct precision daylight bombing against the German war machine's industrial might on the European continent.

During the years 1942, '43, and part of '44, the German occupation of France and the Low Countries was unchallenged. That meant American bombers were open to fighter attack and anti-aircraft fire almost all the way to, and back from, their targets.

The 8th Air Force was effective against the Germans, but that effectiveness came at a price. Many planes and men were lost during this

---

[18] Attleborough is inland from the North Sea at 53° N, 1° E.

period. At the time of Don's arrival in England, only a small percentage of men in the 452nd Bomb Group had made it to twenty-five missions. Twenty-five was the magic number needed to be rotated out of combat duty. When the fighter escorts that accompanied the bombers were eventually fitted with wing tanks sometime during this campaign, they were able to stay with the bombers deeper into the continent. This saved lives. This may have saved Don Morris's life.

Don flew as a togglier on his first six missions. A togglier can best be described as a bombardier fill-in. The bombardier in the squadron's lead plane would drop his load of bombs as the calculations on his Norden bomb sight told him he should. The toggliers in the squadron's other planes would follow the bombardier's lead and drop their loads.

After these first six missions, Don was sent to an eight-day course with a few others. They were trained as radar spot jammers. He flew the rest of his missions as a gunner/spot jammer. The spot jammer manned a receiver and three transmitters. This equipment allowed him to pick up German radar probes and then jam them. Successful jamming would prevent the German anti-aircraft guns from zeroing in on the B-17's exact altitude. As Don explained:

> *Unless we were under fighter attack, I was in the radar room with my three transmitters and my receiver searching for gun laying radar signals and jamming them as fast as I could. When the guys saw me busy, they were sure nervous, as well they might be. The German 88's were sure accurate, and we knew it.*

As Don completed his twenty-five missions, he made the decision to volunteer for another twenty-five mission tour. After a furlough and time at a replacement depot he was assigned to a new crew. He had flown 11 missions with this crew when the war against Germany, or the war in Europe, as it was called, ended. Germany had been defeated.

Because he had volunteered for a second twenty-five mission tour, the Air Corps decided that Don would become part of the Army of Occupation. Quite naturally he wanted to go home. He argued against the occupation assignment to no avail. He was assigned to the 9th

Air Force at Badkissigan, Germany. Here he had a close call with death when flying on a training mission in an A-26 fighter-bomber. This was a three-man plane; pilot and engineer up front and the central fire control gunner (that was Don) in back of the bomb bay.

While flying in formation over France the plane's left engine began to smoke. The last communication Don received over the intercom from the pilot was "gonna abort." The pilot pulled the plane out of formation. For a few minutes everything seemed to be okay. Don received no more communication from up front. Soon a shadow went by him. When a second shadow went by he realized both his crew mates had jumped.

Don opened the door that separated the bomb bay compartment from the cockpit. He saw the auto-pilot blinking at him. By now smoke was pouring out of both engines. He hit the bomb bay door switch so he could exit the plane. The motor groaned but the doors of the bomb bay would not open. He then popped open the small hatch above his head. The opening was only 24-by-24 inches. It was a struggle as Don tried to get himself and his parachute through the opening. He was in a standing position now and he realized that he could reach the bomb bay door switch with his foot. This time the doors began to open. By this time smoke and fire had entered the bomb bay area. Once the opening became large enough, he jumped.

Don's parachute opened, but he broke his left shoulder and his right ankle when he landed in a farm field. He found out later that his pilot and engineer were not so fortunate. Neither of their chutes opened. It was later determined that the pilot's attempt to tell Don to jump was not received because the fire had burned out the intercom.

On September 2, the Japanese signed the treaty of unconditional surrender. The Second World War was now over. In November, Don received his orders to go home. He arrived in the port city of Bologna, France. He found himself stuck there for a number of days while he became part of a company formed of personnel from tank, infantry, air corps, service and supply units. They finally left from La Havre, France, on December 10. They sailed on a Kaiser liberty ship that was part of a convoy of vessels. No sooner had the ships gotten out to sea than they were hit by a vicious storm. Although there was no loss of life, four ships sunk. Don's ship lost a propeller and was towed back to the French coast. Repairs were made and once again the ship sailed for home. On January 7, 1946, the ship took dockage at the Fort Hamilton military facility in Brooklyn, New York. Don's orders then sent him to Hammond, Indiana, where he received his separation orders on January 11. He was the last of the six men in this story to end his regular active duty service.

Like the others in this story, Don Morris, just seventeen years old when his military hitch began, had many experiences and travels in the first half of the 1940s. Despite being a small part of a very massive piece of history, he recalled two incidents that show the world can still be a small place:

> *On a mission to Bremen, Germany, our tail gunner Ken [last name not recalled] took shrapnel in the chest while over the target. We pulled him out of the tail gunner's compartment and applied three compresses to the gaping hole in his chest and covered him as best we could. When we got back to base they took Ken out. We were sure he was dead. No breathing, limbs stiff. He was a goner, for sure.*

A few years later Jack Gray and I made a stop at our favorite watering hole after a softball game. When I looked up there was a guy that looked like Ken, accept [sic] about thirty pounds heavier. I was about to say to Jack, 'That guy looks like', when the guy walks up and says, 'Hi Don'. Jack said later that I turned as white as a sheet. It did take me some time to realize that this was not a ghost. Ken explained that it really was a miracle but he was surely alive. After many months of repairs during which he could not speak or move he finally got home. He had only three-quarters of one lung and one-third of the other. He had eight ribs that were partially rebuilt and much more that I cannot recall. Ken was from Ohio and was in Detroit selling for a Cleveland company.

Don's other story of happenstance involved his long-time family friend, Dave Reed. His story will be told shortly. Dave grew up in the same east side neighborhood as Jim Irvine and Don Morris. For more than forty years after the war the Reed and Morris families were cottage neighbors at their Canadian summer retreat. Don shared a remarkable coincidence about Dave from the war:

Thirty years after the war I made a discovery while sailing my two-man catamaran at Southampton with another ex-G.I., Dave Reed. Dave and I compared notes and discovered that we were on the same convoy attempting to get home in that storm!

Don Morris passed away at age eighty-six in 2012. He was barely twenty-one years old when he returned home from his service time in the Second World War. Like the others in this story, Providence had elected to see him survive.

~~~

Don Morris received the following medals, ribbons and citations for his service:

Distinguished Flying Cross

Air Medal

European-African-Middle Eastern Campaign Medal with three Bronze Campaign Stars

Harry Hurley Hodge

Jim Hodge

Harry Hodge

When twenty-two-year-old Bill Hodge left home for his service in the Marine Corps on February 9, 1942, he left behind his twenty-year-old brother.

Harry Hurley Hodge was born in Lynnville, Tennessee, on October 21, 1921. He is my father.

In April of 1942 Harry tried to enlist in the Marines. He was turned away because he registered high blood pressure in his pre-induction physical. In the years since then high blood pressure was never a problem for dad.

At this time in our story, three of the six men I am writing about were in the Armed Forces. Andy Dixon was at the internment camp in Pomona, California, guarding Japanese Americans; Jim Irvine was finishing cavalry basic training at Fort Riley, Kansas; Bill Hodge was finishing boot camp at Parris Island, South Carolina. By August he would be on Guadalcanal.

Don Morris, who entered the service only twenty-six days before Harry, was still at home.

Harry continued working at his job at Vicker's, where he and Jim Irvine had become friends. Harry continued to date Jim's sister, Jenny, while he waited to be called up in the draft.

The country continued to listen to the radio and read in the newspapers about the war in the struggling days of 1942. Most of the news was bad. Of special interest to the Hodge family was the struggle of the Marines to hold their ground on Guadalcanal Island.

There is no doubt that it was tough for Harry to sit on the sidelines while his brother was on Guadalcanal. Harry Hodge has always had the will to accept his share of the responsibility for things, so it was with a sense of relief when he received his induction notice in January, 1943. He was inducted into the Army on February 3, 1943, at a building in downtown Detroit—serial number 35 566 936. Harry and the others sworn in that day were taken immediately by bus to Michigan

Central Depot. Michigan Central Depot was the train station, at that time the busiest place in Detroit. From there they took the train to what has become a familiar place in this story—Fort Custer near Battle Creek.

This was the beginning of many miles and many places for Harry in the next two years and nine months. Like Don Morris, he was assigned to the Air Corps. That meant moving about to a number of locations in the country as training progressed.

At Fort Custer, Harry and the others were given uniforms and went through various steps of processing. After about one week they were put on a train for St. Petersburg, Florida. This trip took three days.

On arrival in St. Pete, the recruits were put up at the Princess Martha Hotel. In the same way the government used privately owned ships to transport troops, it used privately owned hotels to lodge troops when necessary.

After a week at the Princess Martha, where they underwent further processing, the troops were transported to their nearby tent city. They were really in the Army now, undergoing ten weeks of basic training.

After basic training Harry's orders sent him to Gulfport, Mississippi. Here he went through airplane mechanics school. This training began in June and continued through that summer of 1943. As it turned out, this was training that Harry never used during his time in the Air Corps.

After mechanics school Harry was sent to air gunnery school in the desert outside of Las Vegas, Nevada. It was now September. Harry Hodge and Don Morris came close to being at gunnery school at the same time. They were to become brothers-in-law for more than fifty years, but had met only once or twice prior to the war—most notably when they both stood up in Jim and Marge Irvine's wedding.

Present day Las Vegas is a large city, famed world-wide as a gaudy gambling mecca. Harry remembers it in 1943 as a main street town with an old west flavor to it. Gambling was legal even then, but it wasn't until the 1950s that Las Vegas started its development into a large tourist destination.

After gunnery school Harry was given a furlough. He returned home to Detroit, visiting family, friends and fellow workers at Vickers. He and Jenny Irvine caught up on dating. Jenny knew that when Harry returned to the Air Corps he would be going overseas. As Marge Irvine had her husband gone, Jenny would have her boyfriend gone for an indeterminate time. These were not uncommon situations for many young American women during this era.

After his furlough, Harry's orders sent him to Salt Lake City, Utah. Like Lincoln, Nebraska had been for Don Morris, this was one of the places where the Air Corps formed its ten-man crews for the B-17 bomber. It was here that Harry Hodge became part of a team with some of the young men he would remember best from his war time service. These were the guys, with a couple of changes along the way, with whom he would fly most of his bombing missions in Europe.

The crew of ten was assigned a plane and they flew to Rapid City, South Dakota. Here they trained as a team in both daylight and darkness. As it was with Don Morris, these men had trained with the thirty-caliber machine gun, but now it was the Browning 50-caliber. The enlisted men learned to fire the 50-caliber from each of the B-17's major gun locations: the two waist gun locations, the upper turret, the lower ball turret, and the tail gun locations. The radio man, the bombardier and navigator also each had a gun location. This model B-17 did not a have a chin turret location as some did. The men learned to field strip, break down into serviceable parts, the 50-caliber while in flight—both in daylight and at night.

By January of the new year, 1944, Harry and his crewmates were ready. On or about January 6, they flew from Rapid City to MacDill Field in Tampa-St. Petersburg, Florida. Here they were assigned to the 483rd Bomb Group. It would be their job to get to the 483rd, which was already in Italy. The crew received a final briefing on the risky journey ahead of them.

While at MacDill, Harry had some unfinished business to take care of. He had his mother and Jenny come down by bus from Detroit. He asked Jenny to marry him when he returned from the war. She said yes. He presented her with a ring and their engagement was on. You might say it was a classic war time story. While Harry was flying bombing missions in Europe, Jenny was working the midnight shift at the Briggs plant near her home on Cope Avenue in Detroit. Her job? Riveting wings for bomber aircraft.

From Tampa-St. Pete, Harry's crew flew up to Hunter Field somewhere in southern Georgia. Here they fine-tuned with last minute repairs and a final instrument check.

They then flew to Morrison Field in southern Florida for a full load of fuel. It was from here that the plane, piloted by Lieutenant Edward Promberger of Pocahantas, Arkansas, left the U.S.A.

In this age of computers, jet aircraft, and instantaneous communication, it may seem strange that in 1944 so much was involved just to get to southern Europe. Yet it was a different time then, with different technology.

The crew flew to the island of Trinidad to top off their fuel tanks. Then it was on to Belem, Brazil.[19] This is a fair-sized city just south of the mighty Amazon River, not far from the Atlantic Ocean. Harry remembers the airfield being surrounded by the jungle. Here the plane was refueled again.

A look at the map shows why the B-17s destined for southern Europe left from this place to cross the Atlantic. Here was one of the closest

---

[19] Belem, Brazil is at 20° S, 48° W.

jumping off points between the Americas and the closest point of land on the African continent—the city of Dakar,[20] in the country of Senegal. The four-engine B-17, properly navigated, could make the trip to Dakar on a full load of fuel.

The twin engine planes—the fighters, fighter/bombers and some twin-engine bombers, all with fuel capacities less than the B-17—took off from a location farther south in Brazil. This was done so that these smaller planes could land at Asuncion Island, a speck of land in the middle of the South Atlantic, where they could be refueled. The Americans mispronounced it "Ascension." Hitting this small island require exact navigation. The saying was, "If you missed Ascension your wife got a pension."

The trip from Belem to Dakar went smoothly. Harry's crew spent overnight at the airfield in Dakar for refueling and any repairs. They then took off, traveling north across the western edge of the huge Sahara desert. Destination: Marrakech, Morocco.

---

[20] Dakar is at 15° N, 12° W.

Harry recollects that they were at the airfield in Marrakech for five or six days. They then took off north-northeast, crossing the Mediterranean Sea, for Foggia, Italy. A number of airfields around Foggia[21] were home to the American 15th Air Force. It was from Foggia that Harry's crew would fly bombing missions as part of the 483rd Bomb Group.

Harry and Bill Hodge, and their younger sister Hilda, never had much as youngsters, yet dad's comments about what he saw in Africa and Italy, showed how well-off life was back home:

> *It was a very different way of life for the people who live there compared to the lifestyle of the citizens in the U.S.A. All the one's we saw appeared to be very poor. I have no idea how they made a living other than to farm to some degree. I think at this point a lot of those people might have lived off whatever they could salvage from the spoils of war or off the American Army.*

On first arriving in Foggia the crew was attached to the 99th Bomb Group. The airfield that would be home to the 483rd was not yet completed. In all the comments and written

---

[21] Foggia is inland from the Adriatic Sea at 15° N, 16° degrees E.

information my father provided to me, the most telling is his comments about his first mission:

> *Our crew was split up when we flew our first mission from there and on that day the C.O. [Commanding Officer] of the 99th was shot down. I remember feeling this was the most exhausting day of my life. I guess it was the newness of it all. From now on it was all business.*

As the weeks and months passed the 483rd Bomb Group, and the 15th Air Force as a whole, did its best to disrupt and destroy German operations in eastern Europe. They hit targets in Romania, Austria, Hungary, Italy, Bulgaria, the Balkans and southern Germany. The most consistently hit targets were the oil fields around Ploesti, Romania.[22]

Being on a bombing crew was work of extremes. While not on a mission airman lived in safety and comfort compared to ground troops. While on a bombing mission the airmen were doing the duty with the highest risk of loss of life.

---

[22] Ploesti is approximately seventy-five miles north of Bucharest, at 42° N, 26° E.

On most bomb runs, the B-17s would leave Foggia, cross the Adriatic Sea, travel over the mountains of the Balkans, and head to the specific target. A significant landmark on many missions was the Danube River. Here the umbrella of fighter escort protection returned to Foggia because of fuel limitations. The Germans knew this so the bombers would not come under fighter attack until they crossed the Danube. In the case of the oil fields, that meant 175 miles to the target and 175 miles back to the Danube without fighter escort. As mentioned in Don Morris's story, the fighters were eventually fitted with wing tanks. That meant the protection of fighter escort all the way to the oil fields and back.

Elements of the 15th Air Force, including the 483rd Bomb Group, carried out the first shuttle run into Russia. This operation was known as the "Poltava Affair." The target, Debrecen, Hungary, was so far from Foggia that the bombers could not carry enough fuel to return to Foggia after hitting the target. The Germans knew that their facility at Debrecen was safe from attack.

By this time in the war, the Union of Soviet Socialist Republics—the Soviet Union—had become our ally. American and Soviet intelligence worked together to allow the American bombers to fly east into Ukraine to land and refuel after hitting Debrecen. The B-17s landed at a number of different air strips around the city of Poltava. This caught the Germans completely by surprise.

Harry's plane, and the rest of the 483rd, landed on the vast Ukrainian steppe at the village of Myrhorod. He recalls that they were there for five or six days. Mechanics had flown on the mission to make necessary repairs.

The Americans saw some of the devastation in the area while they were there. The Germans had occupied this area and had been driven out by the Soviets in earlier weeks. As they retreated, the Germans employed their "scorched earth" policy.

It is worth noting that while the Americans were there, the Allies launched the June 6 D-day invasion of continental Europe.

During their stay in Mryhorod, the 483rd made a bombing run to Galati, Romania, using Soviet bombs. In great part, because they caught the Germans by surprise, this shuttle mission, the "Poltava Affair", was successful. For good measure, on their way back to Foggia the planes hit a target at Focsani, Romania.

For Harry Hodge and Don Morris, a piece of happenstance accompanied the Air Corps "Poltava Affair." After the 15th Air Force's success in the initial shuttle run a second run was flown, this time from England. This was an 8th Air Force operation and guess who was on that mission? Yes, it was Don Morris. I quote from his correspondence to me regarding this mission:

> *On a shuttle mission we bombed Berlin and continued on to Poltava, Russia [now Ukraine]. From there we were to refuel, take on Russian bombs and be given another target to bomb on the way back to England. The first part went fairly well. We hit Berlin and continued on to Poltava with not much trouble. That evening the Luftwaffe paid us a visit, destroying forty-four of our planes on the ground.*

The Germans had caught on quickly. The planes of the 8th Air Force paid a heavy price for being the second ones to employ the shuttle operation.

By late August, Harry reached the goal of having flown fifty missions. This meant rotation out of flying bombing missions. You will notice that duty in the 15th Air Force required twice the number of missions flown for rotation as did the 8th Air Force in Britain. The attrition rate was greater in the 8th so the airmen of the 15th were required to fly twice as many missions.

In looking through some of dad's papers and keepsakes from his time in the 483rd Bomb Group I discovered that he kept some bomb tags from some of the missions he flew on. A bomb tag is nothing more than a cotter pin with a sturdy paper tag on it. The paper tag has an instruction on it that says not to remove the tag until the bomb's fuse is put in place. The fuses were put in place when the bombs were being loaded on a plane for a mission. Harry would then take one of the discarded tags, save it, and later write a sentence or two about the mission. The tag for his last mission says the following: "August 25, 24,000 ft. Target: Airfield and A/C factory. The target was hit very well. Heavy flak over target. I flew tail gunner and did I sweat as it was my last mission."

The target that day was Bronzola, Italy.

Harry's orders now sent him back to the States. He and his crew mate and friend Johnny Farrell both shipped back on an Army ship that was manned by the Navy. There were roughly sixty returning airmen on this ship. There were also a number of German prisoners of war on board. The returning airmen were assigned guard duty over these prisoners. According to Harry, this consisted of nothing more than taking turns standing guard with a shotgun at the hatch leading to the ship's hold where the prisoners were kept.

Harry Hodge hit U.S. soil sometime around October 4. His orders had him report to Fort Dix, New Jersey. From there he was sent to Chicago, and then he was given a three-week furlough. Harry and Jenny decided to get married during this furlough. The wedding was planned and executed within two weeks. I remember my Aunt Hilda fondly commenting on how quickly and without fuss that this wedding was put together.

Tech. Sgt. Harry Hodge and Jenny Irvine were married on October 19, 1944. Harry's brother Bill, his new brother-in-law Jim Irvine, and his friend Andy Dixon were not able to attend the wedding. They, along with Don Morris and the next man in this story, Dave Reed, were still scattered in other parts of the world. In the wedding party, however, was Harry's friend and B-17 crew mate, Johnny Farrell.

After a four day honeymoon Harry's orders had him report to Miami, Florida. John Farrell had the same orders. They traveled down to Miami by bus. The Army put them up at the Madison Hotel on Collins Avenue—right in the heart of Miami's resort district. It seemed the Army Air Corps didn't know what to do with them for a couple of weeks.

Hodge and Farrell then received orders to report to Laredo Army Air Base in Laredo, Texas. Harry took a troop train to Texas, while John got a "delay in route" to return to Detroit where he had his own car. He brought his wife Betty and Jenny Hodge down to Laredo in his Packard automobile.

The trip to Laredo by car was nothing in itself to be taken for granted. Gasoline during the war was strictly rationed. In reflecting back on this trip, Harry was not sure how his buddy got the gas ration cards to make the trip.

In Laredo, Harry served as a gunnery instructor for new airmen. This was mostly classroom instruction where the airmen learned about the fifty-caliber machine gun.

Christmas came and went and 1944 came to a close. It had been quite a couple of years for Harry Hodge. He had been at seventeen locations on four continents, had crossed the Atlantic Ocean twice, was credited with fifty-two bombing missions against the Germans, had gotten married and was about to father his first child. Quite a couple of years for a young man who, as a youngster, thought Outer Drive Avenue in the city of Detroit was a long way out.

In January, Harry received orders for "airman and wife" to report to Westover Air Base near Chicopee Falls, Massachusetts. On the train to Massachusetts Jenny did not feel well at all. In Chicopee Falls the doctor let her know that she was expecting her first child. That would be me, the writer of this story. By April, it was thought best for Jenny to return to Detroit to be under her own doctor's care and under the watchful care of her mother.

On May 8, Germany surrendered. On September 2, Japan surrendered. The Second World War was over.

Harry was separated from the military service on September 26 at Westover Air Base. Time of service was two years, seven months and sixteen days. Mustering out pay was $300.00.

The next day Harry arrived at Michigan Central Depot in Detroit. He soon arrived at the

Irvine home to be with Jenny and the two-week-old son he had yet to see. When Harry's mother-in-law, Liz Irvine, opened the door for Harry, I am told she was carrying me under her arm like a sack of potatoes. You have already read of the great coincidence of that day in Jim Irvine's story.

Harry Hodge, like the others in this story, had met his obligation and now had come home.

~~~

Harry Hodge received the following medals, ribbons and citations for his service:

    Good Conduct Medal

    Presidential Unit Citation

    European African Middle Eastern Theater Campaign Ribbon with five Battle Stars

    Air Medal with four Oak Leaf Clusters

Jim Hodge

David Charles Read

Jim Hodge

Dave Reed

A common practice of people of the British Isles, and those in America of that nationality, is to borrow the relationship terms "aunt" and "uncle" and apply them to the dearest of friends, so that their children learned to call these friends by these terms of endearment. Such is the case for me, my brothers and my cousins regarding Aunt Jean and Uncle Dave Reed.

The Reeds have been friends of the Irvines, and subsequently their spouses, since their youth. It is a privilege to recognize Uncle Dave Reed's military contribution during World War II.

Dave was awarded the second highest medal that can be achieved by an American soldier—the Silver Star.

The inscription accompanying his Silver Star reads:

Technician Sgt. Grade David C. Reed 365 41 007

Serial # Co. D, 21st Tank Battalion, US Army. For gallantry in action at Fischbach, Germany on 20, March 1945.

Technician 4th Grade Reed, a tank driver, materially aided in repulsing a sudden enemy attack by braving intense hostile fire to operate an exposed tank turret machine gun throughout the attack, killing and wounding many of the enemy. His gallant achievement reflects great credit upon himself and the military forces of the United States.

Entered service from Detroit.

Dave's unit was part of General George Patton's Third Army. Patton's army raced to relieve American troops at the Battle of the Bulge. This is when Dave earned his Silver Star. My father and my Uncle Don never remember him speaking of the medal, or the events that led to the medal.

Dave Reed's unit also liberated the Dachau Concentration Camp. Dachau was one of a number of such camps where the German Nazi Party had rounded up and systematically murdered European Jews. One can imagine the impact on Dave and his fellow soldiers when they came upon this place of atrocity.

Dave's son Don, now retired from his own career in the Air Force, has told me that when his mother and father visited his family in Germany a number of years ago, they went to the Dachau memorial. Don said his father's face was ashen during this visit.

~~~

Dave Reed received the following medals, ribbons and citations for his service:

    Silver Star

    WW II Victory Service Medal

    Good Conduct Medal

    American Campaign Ribbon

    European-African-Middle Eastern Campaign Ribbon (EAME)

My Father and My Uncles

Jim Hodge

In the Passing Years

Seventy-nine years have passed since these men completed their active military service at the end of the Second World War. Through a sibling relationship, and through marriages that began even during the war, they became connected to help form a large extended family.

Andy Dixon came back to Detroit, and in 1946 he married Bill and Harry Hodge's sister, Hilda. Andy and Hilda had one daughter in 1947. In 1950 they had a second daughter who lived only a few hours.

Andy renewed his relationship with the Army when he took a civil service job at the

Army's 70th Reserve Division in Livonia, Michigan, later in his working life. This was the work from which he retired.

My brothers and I were thought of like sons by Uncle Andy. He enjoyed sharing his love for hunting and fishing with us. We have fond memories of such times with him during the 1950s and 60s.

Andy passed away in 1986. He was sixty-nine years old.

Jim Irvine went on to touch the lives of many people. He and Marge had eight children. He realized his goal of becoming an engineer and he worked diligently at that career until he retired.

Uncle Jim's dry sense of humor and his low-key, sincere emotion were trademarks. He always retained his driving competitive edge on the playing field of any sport. We shared great times watching him on the softball diamond and playing golf with him. His excuses for a poor golf shot or a poor round of golf were legendary. We shared many laughs over his list of excuses. He was one of the cornerstones of the good times that my brothers, my cousins, and I enjoyed at our summer retreat in Canada.

Jim Irvine was a physically rugged man but, as will be for all of us, his body eventually shut down. He passed away in April of 1999. He was seventy-eight years old.

Bill Hodge remained an officer in the Marine Reserve until 1952. In his new life in Eagle River, Wisconsin, he served as a Marine recruiting officer in his spare time. When the Korean War broke out in 1950 Bill would have most certainly been called up for active duty except for the scars from his time on Guadalcanal—recurring malaria and loss of hearing in one ear. The ear infection that the Guadalcanal Marines called jungle rot plagued Bill for the rest of life. He had to have his ear cleaned out twice a year.

Bill and Gloria had one daughter. The couple divorced and Bill moved back to Detroit later in the 1950s. In 1959 he married Pauline Orton. They were blessed with three children.

Bill was a career carpenter. He and Pauline retired in South Lyon, Michigan. In that retirement he became somewhat of a local legend as the town handyman.

Bill passed away at the age of ninety in 2010.

Don Morris married Elsie Irvine, youngest sister of Jim Irvine, in 1952. They had three children. Don retired from the Detroit Fire Department.

We have included a few wartime coincidences or ironies throughout this story. Don had one as a fire fighter as well. He was called to a fire one night at the house where he had been born.

Don passed away in 2012. He was eighty-six years old. Elsie continues to own the cottage at Southampton, Ontario, Canada, that she and Don bought more than fifty years ago. Many in our extended family still enjoy occasional trips to Southampton. A stop or two at the Morris cottage has always been a must.

Harry Hodge was always what he sometimes called in others a "hard charger."

Always an optimist, always a can-do outlook. He stayed busy in his retirement; constantly improving, with Jenny, their Michigan home. He fashioned beautiful things in wood for the homes of his daughters-in-law. He also created keepsakes for his grandchildren and great-grandchildren.

Harry and Jenny had sixty-two years of marriage together. They had three sons, including the writer of this story. Although increased distances separated us as the years passed, we all tried our best to arrive at mom and dad's for Christmas Eve. For years we enjoyed gathering for backyard summer cookouts on their wooden patio deck—built by Harry, of course.

Harry passed away in 2021. He lived to be one-hundred years old.

Dave Reed always retained his easy-going personality. He seemed never to get ruffled. His fine singing voice, a common trait of his Welsh heritage, was a pleasure to listen to. He worked diligently with his brother-in-law, and eventually one of his sons, in the family barber shop.

We lost this good man much too early. Uncle Dave suffered a fatal heart attack while driving alone on his way to be with Aunt Jean at their cottage in Southampton, Ontario, in 1980. He was fifty-nine years old.

~~~

We can be grateful that these six men all survived their risky journeys in the Second World War. Their efforts, and the efforts of sixteen million other American veterans, have allowed us to enjoy the freedom that we too often take for granted. That is good news for all of us.

And regarding these six men, there is more good news. Each of them, somewhere along the way in their life, accepted the Christian Gospel. Many things may change in this world as the years go by, but God's offer to us will not change.

The Second World War was a time of great heartache and tragedy. Yet, as is the way of the human spirit, there was much to be cherished for these men and their families. Someday the Second World War will be as distant to the future reader of this story as the Civil War is to us living now. May this family history serve us all well in remembering.

Jim Hodge

The Next Generation

Twenty years after my father and uncles returned from their service in World War II, I entered the service during the Vietnam era.

I attended college for a year, but had no real goal in mind. More than that, I felt that my life would always have something missing in it if I did not serve my country somewhere in the armed services. So, I volunteered for the draft in 1965.

I entered the Army in June of that year. After basic training, the Army sent me to Fort Sam Huston, Texas, where I went through ten weeks of training to become a medic.

We all thought for sure that we were headed to Vietnam, but they shipped us off to Korea instead. The garden spot, they called it.

My Father and My Uncles

Despite our medic training most of us were transferred to the infantry. My 2nd Division brigade wound up along the border—the Demilitarized Zone, or the DMZ.

The Korean War had wound up in a bitter stalemate and truce in 1953. A jagged three-mile-wide buffer zone, the DMZ, was established right where the fighting stopped. It ran all the way across the Korean peninsula. A one or two strand barbed wire mounted on metal stakes was the demarcation line. It split the DMZ: a mile-and-a-half for each warring side. It was a no-man's land where only so many military personnel, so much equipment, and only small arms weapons were allowed—as begrudgingly agreed to at the truce talks.

We ran patrols in the DMZ and we had four observation posts in our battalion's sector of responsibility. These observation posts—small wooden huts on prominent hilltops—were surrounded by cyclone fencing, concertina barbed wire, and claymore mines. Eight to ten men spent a twenty-four-hour shift at an observation post. They watched us and we watched them.

My experience in Korea allowed me to better appreciate the experiences of my father and my uncles. For all those who have, and continue to, serve our nation in the military service—often inspired by the service of their own family members—I say thank you for your service to our nation.

J. H.

My Father and My Uncles

Appendix A

WWII Mission Journal of Harry Hodge

In 2017, at age ninety-six, my father began to slip mentally. With my mother having passed away in 2006, I became dad's primary care giver. Along with keeping his financial and medical affairs in order, I became caretaker of their lifetime of memorabilia. Amongst dad's wartime material I found a treasure that I had no idea existed. It is a journal that he kept during the war describing some his missions.

These accounts were jotted down with pencil after each mission. It begins with Harry's twenty-fifth mission and runs through his fiftieth mission.

It should be noted that sometimes credit for two missions is given on the same day's operation. This is determined on a formula the Air Corps used based on a number of criteria, such as target hits, length of flight, enemy fighter encounters, extreme weather conditions, and so on.

The mission journal is in remarkable condition for its age and the conditions in which it was originally written. It is presented the with occasional corrections by my father, as best as I have been able to decipher his handwriting. He printed in capital letters, but I have not followed that for ease of readability.

Also, my father did not finish high school until after the war. His grammar and spelling are not as polished as they were later in his life. I have kept my own editing to a minimum so as to not interrupt the flow of his thoughts.

Photos of the actual pages are as nearly as possible facing the text. Blank pages have not been reproduced.

The cover depicts a plane surrounded by flak, with a man dropping a bomb. The face is erased. I do not know why.

Below my father's drawing is his explanation about the start date: "I GUESS I DID NOT START TO MAKE NOTES UNTIL MISSION #25 ON JUNE 22 1944."

As all military do, my father had his technical terms and slang. For the benefit of the reader clarification of a few words my father used follow:

Box: The four plane rectangular formation in which each squadron flew.

B.T.: Ball turret. A rotatable machine gun position on the top and/or belly of the B-17.

Chaff: Light weight metallic material that, when thrown out of the B-17, helped to disorient the enemy's anti-aircraft guns from zeroing in on the B-17's altitude.

Feather: To slow down, or shut down, one of the B-17's prop engines.

Flak: The shrapnel from a detonated anti-aircraft shell.

Fort: The Flying Fortress B-17.

G.P.: General purpose

H-hour: Pre-flight briefing hour.

I.P.: Initial point: The spot where the bomb run would begin.

Jerrys: Slang. Referring to Germans.

Milk run: An easy mission.

Pathfinder: The lead plane in the lead box. The group lead navigator is in this plane. The group holds its formation based on the pathfinder plane. Especially critical in heavy cloud cover.

P-38 & P-51: American fighter aircraft.

P.B.Y.: A plane that specialized in scouting, as well as search and rescue.

Jim Hodge

My Father and My Uncles

Jim Hodge

WWII Mission Journal of Harry Hodge

MISSION NO. 25   JUNE 22, 1944
                                    N. ITALY
OUR TARGET TODAY WAS THE MARSHALLING YARDS AT FORNOVRAITARO HAD A LATE H-HOUR THIS MORNING. ALSO HAD A VERY ROUGH MISSION WHICH WAS SUPPOSED TO BE A "MILK RUN."

OUR CREW B/S FLEW WITH OUR C.O. CAPT. LOUIS T. SEITH, OUR OWN FIRST PILOT, LT. E. R. PROMBERGER AS CO-PILOT. CAPT. HARREN AS BOMBADEER, AS OUR BOMB. FOR THIS MISSION, A LT. DIAMOND AS NAVIGATOR. IT WAS OUR FIRST MISSION WITH ANY OF THESE OFFICERS, WITH THE EXCEPTION OF LT. PROMBERGER.

TAKE OFF AT ABOUT 0900. WE FLED FLEW NO 3 BOX, NO 1 POSITION.

MISSION WENT VERY WELL UP TO & OVER THE TARGET. THERE WAS A WORLD OF SMOKE OVER THE TARGET AT THE TIME OF BOMBS AWAY CALL. WE WERE LOADED WITH TWENTY 250 LBS. G.P. BOMBS. I WAS LOOKING THRO THE GLASSES AND SAW TERRIFIC EXPLOSIONS AND BRIGHT ORANGE & RED FLASHES. OUR BOX HIT THE OIL TANK & YARDS TOGETHER.

THERE WAS NO FLAK GOING TO OR OVER THE TARGET. THE LEFT WAIST GUNNER & MYSELF BOTH REMOVED OUR FLAK SUITES VERY SHORTLY AFTER LEAVING TARGET AREA, A PRATICE USUALLY NOT EMPLOYED BY EITHER OF US.

ON OUR RETURN TRIP WE WERE BRIEFED ON APPROX. 12 FLAK GUNS NEAR BOLANO, ITALY RATHER SOUTH OF IT. WE SAW A BIT OF FLAK AT 12:30 & 1 O'CLOCK POSITION. WE ATTEMPED TO AVOID THIS FLAK AND IN DOING SO WE TURNED DIRECTLY INTO THE BATTERYS OF BOLANO. IT SEEMS THAT THE JERRIES WERE VERY SMART AND FIRED THOSE FIRST BURSTS ON OUR RIGHT WINGS, IN HOPES WE WOULD TURN LEFT TO PUT MORE DISTANCE BETWEEN US AND THE FLAK. WE FULFILLED THEIR HOPES. PERSONALLY I DONT KNOW IF IT WAS ANY OF THOSE GUNS

Jim Hodge

Mission No. 25   June 22, 1944

Our target today was the marshalling yards at Fornova, Di taro N. Italy. Had a late H-hour this morning, 0610. Also had a very rough mission which was supposed to be a "milk run."

Our crew 810 flew with our C.O. Capt. Louis T. Seith, our own first pilot, Lt. E.R. Promberger as co-pilot. Capt. Harrell, sqd. bombardier, as our bomb – for this mission, & Lt. Diamond as navigator. It was our first mission with any of these officers, with the exception of Lt. Promberger.

Take off at about 09:00. We flew No 3 box, No 1 position.

Mission went very well up to & over the target. There was a world of smoke over the target at the time of our bombs away call. We were loaded with twenty, 250 lbs. G.P. bombs. I was looking thru the glasses and saw terrific explosions and bright orange & red flashes. Our box hit the oil tank & yard together.

There was no flak going to or over the target. The left waist gunner & myself removed our flak suites very shortly after leaving target area, a practice usually not employed by either of us.

On our return trip we were briefed on aprrox. 12 flak guns near Bolono, Italy rather south of it. We saw a bit of flak at 12:30 - 1 O'clock position. We attempted to avoid this flak and in doing so we turned directly into the batterys of

My Father and My Uncles

Bolono. It seems that the Jerrys were very smart and fired those first bursts on our right wings in hopes we would turn left to put more distance between us and the flak. We fullfilled their hopes. Personally, I don't know who was at fault but they were briefed on those guns.

> This is what happed. When we turned left to avoid the flak we actually flew down a path towards their guns. Before we knew it we were in "Flak Alley." Most of it was still on our right, in fact in looked like thousands of bursts out there getting blacker & closer each second. I could not help looking at it, (as everyone else seemed to feel the same,) we liked to get away from it, but at the same time you can't help but watch it.
>
> I suddenly saw a ship (his sqd) at approx 4 o'clock. It did a little dip & fell off on the right wing. No #4 eng. was feathered at the time. It maintained this position for a few seconds, and during this time two small objects flew away from her. I believe they were two of the three escape panels. Then I saw one man leap clear. Our B.T. man said his chute opened in a delayed jump. The ship then did a wing over and started to spin. At the same time another man cleared the ship, his chute opening promptly. By now she was spinning, and a fire was very visible in the section of No 4 engine. The fire continued to grow and a few seconds later the right wing blew off. It appeared to take the larger portion of the this assembly with it. By now there were huge bks of orange flame engulfing them. The sections of the ship (there were reports of two or three chts seen after the exp.) I sure hope so.
>
> I watched the falling remains and the large section was the left wing & part of the fuselage. It struck the ground with a terrific force.

122

This is what happed. When we turned left to avoid the flak we actually flew down a path towards their guns. Before we knew it we were in "flak ally." Most of it was still on our right, in fact it looked like thousands of bursts out there getting blacker and closer each second. I could not help looking at it, (as everyone else seemed to feel the same.) We like to hide from it, but at the same time, you cain't help but watch it.

I suddenly saw a ship (815 sqd) at approx 4 o clock. It did a little dip & fell of[f] on the right wing. No 4 eng. was feathered at the time. It maintained this position for a few seconds, and during this time two small objects flew away from her. I believe they were two of the three escape panels. Then I saw one man leap clear. Our B.T. man said his chute opened in a delayed jump. The ship then did a wing over and started to spin. At the same time another man cleared the ship, his shute opening promptly. By now she was spinning, and a fire was very visible in the section of No 4 engine. The fire [continued] to grow and a few seconds later the right wing blew off. It appeared to take the larger portion of the tai[l] assembly with it. By now there were huge balls of orange flame engulfing the sections of the ship. (There were reports of two or three chuts seen after the exp.) I sure hope so.

I watched the falling remains and the largest section was the left wing and part of the fuselage. It struck the ground with a terrific force.

Mission #25   (pg. 3)

That ship came from the box ahead. The box
C/Maj. Reakdon was the unlucky one. Two of his
ships were knocked out. One being the one which
blew up. I believe the other one was the ship
I saw close to the water later on. It was
reported to have ditched & P.B.Y. sent after it.
Claims say that another ship is still missing.
None of our sqd's ships or boys hit I understand.

Upon landing there was heck of a mess.
One ship before us ran off the end of
the runway, no brakes. (Good job of landing).
Our sqd ship, pilot "Left McNary." After we
landed a ship ran off the leeside of
runway. I don't know the trouble. Also a
ship ran off the r.w. near the landing end.
It ruined landing gear, I understand. The four-
                              no brake pressure up.
ship could not get her gear down so she
circled for a while until fixed. Upon landing
I supposed her brakes failed for she
ran off the runway close to the colored
guard area. (Landing time 14:10) Sage + 10 mins fly
                                      for the group
For a supposed "milk run" today, we ended
up with lots of hard luck. Thank goodness
this does not happen each mission. I hope
pray it never happens again in any form.

Mission #25 (pg.3)

That ship came from the box ahead. The box of Maj. Reardon was the unlucky one. Two of his ships were knocked out. One being the one which blew up. I believe the other one was the ship that we saw close to the water later on. It was reported to have ditched & a P.B.Y. sent after it.

Claims say that another ship is still missing. None of our sqd's ships or boys hit I understand.

Upon landing there was a heck of a mess. One ship before us ran off the end of the runway; no brakes. (A good job of landing). (815 sqd ship, pilot "Capt. MS. Narry.")[23] After we landed a ship ran off the left side of the runway. I don't know the trouble. Also a ship ran off the r.w. near the landing end. It ruined it's landing gear. I understand, the fourth ship could not get her hyd. brake pressure up, so she circled for a while until fixed. Upon landing I suppose her brakes failed for she ran of[f] the runway close to the colored guard area. (Landing time 14:10) (5 hrs & 16 mins flight for the group)

For a supposed "milk run" today, we ended up with lots of hard luck. Thank goodness this does not happen each mission. I hope and pray it never happens again in any form.

---

[23] The name could possibly be Capt. McNarry.

My Father and My Uncles

MISSION #26 & 27   JUNE 23, 1944

OUR TARGET TODAY WAS THE OIL REFINERIES AT PLOESTIA ROMANIA. (SECONDARY TARGET WAS THE CITY ITSELF) WHICH ? BOMBED.

HAD A VERY EARLY H-HOUR THIS MORNING. 03:00. TO START OFF WITH MOST OF US DID NOT FEEL TO GOOD.

OUR CREW 8/8 FLEW WITH S/SGT BILL HESTER AS REPLACEMENT ? GEORGE STOVALL, OUR B.T. MAN. THE OFFICERS INCLUDED OR PILOT 2ND LT. E.R. PROMBERGER, 1ST LT. WAYNE, 1ST GEORGE AS BOMBDIER WEBER, 1ST KEYS, AS NAVIGATOR.

WE FLEW No 4 POS IN THE LEAD BOX, LEADING THE GROUP. FOUR BOMB GPS BOMBED THE TARGET.

THINGS WENT WELL AND OUR 2-2000 LB + 2-1000 LB. BOMBS WENT AWAY WELL. THE OIL REFINERIES WERE UNDER A THICK OVERCAST AND THE PATH FINDER C??D NOT PICK THEM UP. WE SIGHTED & BOMBED THE CITY OF   ITSELF. I UNDERST THEY MADE GOOD HITS.

ON THE BOMB RUN THERE WAS A LARGE AMOUNT OF FLAK COMING UP AT US. THE OTHER WAIST GUNNER + MYSELF WERE VERY BUSY THROWING OUT CHAFF. I COULD SEE A LOT OF FLAK BURSTS BENEATH US. AT FIRST THEY WERE LOW BUT BEGAN TO CLIMB UP TOWARD US. AT THE SAME TIME THERE WAS A GREAT VOLUME FLAK UP TO OUR SIDES I SAW ??? JUST A LITTLE O? THIS, DUE TO THROWING OUT THE CHAFF. (AFTER WE LE? THE TARGET I SAW A HUGE WALL OF BLACK, WHERE ??D BEEN.)

Jim Hodge

Mission #26 & 27   June 23, 1944

Our target today was the oil refineries at Polestia [Ploiesti] Romania (secondary target was the city itself) which we bombed.

Had a very early H-Hour this morning. 03:00. To start it off with most of us did not feel to good.

Our crew 810, flew with s/sgt. Bill Nester as replacement. To George Stovall, our B.T. man. The officers inculded [included] our pilot 2nd. Lt. E.R. Promberger, 1st Lt. Wayne, 1st George Swerer, as bombadier, 1st Keys, as navigator.

We flew No 4 pos in the lead box, leading the group. Four bomb gps. bombed the target.

Things went well and our 2-2,000 lb & 2-1,000 lb. bombs went away well. The oil refineries were under a thick over cast and the path finder did not pick them up. He sighted & bombed the city of [blank space]^{24} itself. I understand they made good hits.

On the bomb ron [run] there was a large amount of flak coming up at us. The other waist gunner and my self were very busy throwing out chaff. I could see a lot of flack bursts beneath us. At first they were low but began to climb up towards us. At the same time there was a great volume of flak off to our sides. I saw just a little of this,

---

^{24} Blank space in the original. He evidently did not know the name of the city. It may have been Ploiesti, Romania, as he mentioned in an earlier entry.

due to throwing out the chaff. (After we left the target I saw a hogh [huge] wall of black, where we had been.)

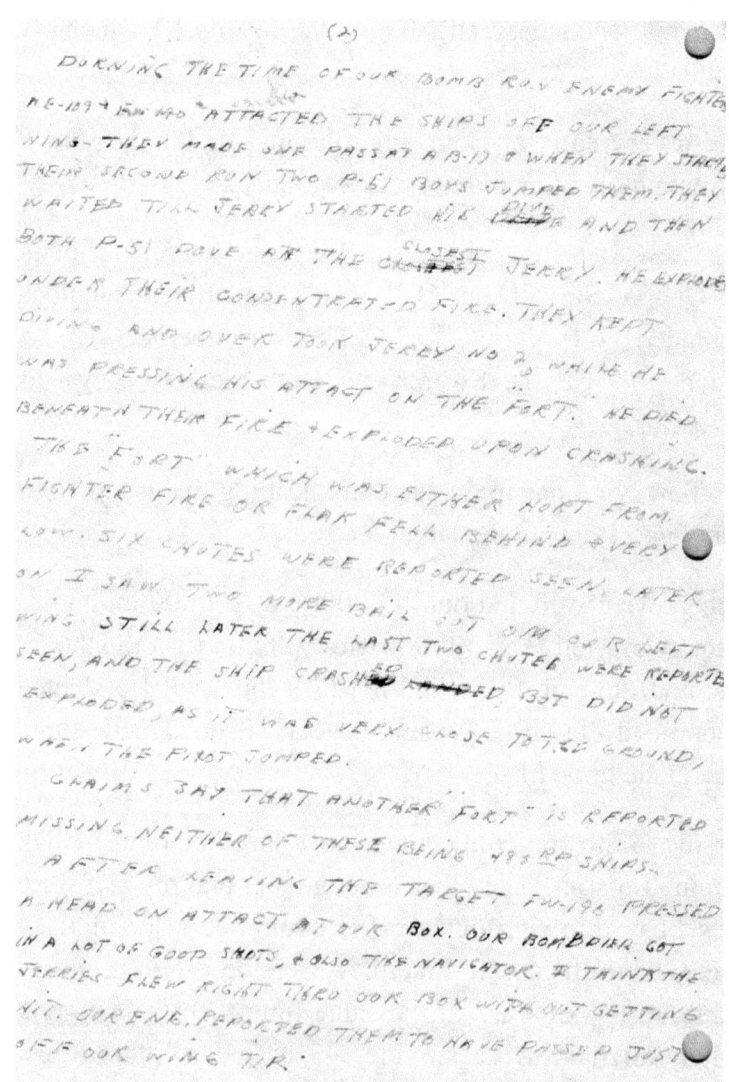

(2)

Durning [During] the time of our bomb run enemy fighters me-109 & ew 4-9-0 attacked the ships off our left wing - they made one pass at a B-17 & when they started their second run two P-51 boys jumped them. They waited till Jerry started his dive and then both P-51 dove at the closest Jerry. He exploded under their consentrated fire. They kept diving and over took Jerry No 2, while he was pressing his attack on the "Fort". He died beneath their fire & exploded upon crashing.

The "Fort" which was hort [hurt] from fighter fire or flak fell behind & very low. Six chutes were reported seen. Later on I saw two more bail out on our left wing. Still later the last two chutes were reported seen, and the ship crashed, but did not exploded, as it was very close to the ground, when the pilot jumped.

Claims say that another "Fort" is reported missing, neither of these being 483rd ships.

After leaving the target FW-190 pressed ahead on attact [attack] at our box. Our bombdier got in a lot of good shots, & also the navigator. I think the Jerries flew right thru our box with out getting hit. Our eng. Reported them to have passed just off our wing tip.

(3) MISSION # 26 ???

We had left the flak area and the B.T. man
pointed gasoline leaking from behind No 3 eng.
I could smell it strongly, even with our oxygen
masks on. The pilot feathered No 3 & the eng.
attempted to transfer the fuel, but the pumps
would not operate. The gas was leaking rather
badly and continued to do so for some time.
Our pilot suggested starting No 3 eng again
and in spite of cautioning from Lt. Waxing he
attempted to unfeather No 3 prop. Thank heaven
it would not unfeather, because there was a very
very good chance for the eng. to throw sparks back
into the wing with gas & vapors in it. It may
not mean much, but the failing of the prop.
to unfeather may have saved us a lot of
grief.

We maintained our position & came in on three
good engines, which is plenty of power. Upon
landing we found the flak hole to be beneath
the feeder tank of No 3 eng, & of about 5 five or
six inches long. The gas was still leaking
but not quiet so badly. (Landing time 13:45)
All in all it was a long flight 7 hrs & 45 mins
might have turned out differently if the No 3 prop that
?? that fire out and ??

(3)

Mission # 26 & 27

We had left the flak area and the B.T. man reported gasoline leaking from behind No 3 eng. We could smell it strongly, even with our oxygen masks on. The pilot feathered. No 3 & the eng. attempted to transfer the fuel, but the pumps would not operate. The gas was leaking rather badly and continued to do so for some time

Our pilot suggested starting No 3 eng again, and in spite of cautioning from Lt. Wayne he attempted to unfeather No 3 prop. Thank heavens it would not unfeather, because there was a very very good chance for the eng. to throw sparks back into the wing with gas & vapors in it. It may not mean much, but the failing of the prop, to unfeather may have saved us a lot of grief.

We maintained our position & came in on three good engines, which is plenty of power. Upon landing we found the flak hole to be beneath the feeder tank of No 3 eng, of about five or six inches long. The gas was still leaking but not quiet [quite] so badly. (landing time 13:45)

All in all it was a long flight 7 hrs & 45 mins which might have turned out differently if the No 3 prop had unfeathered. We reall[y] sweat that ride out and thank

(7).
HEAVENS FOR OUR BLESSINGS.

Jim Hodge

(4)

heavens for our blessings.

MISS.ON N° 28   JUNE 25,1944
                 CARBIMATION
OUR TARGET TODAY WAS THE MARSHALLING YARDS,
SUB BASES, AND OIL STORAGE TANKS AT SETE FRANCE.
IT WAS STRICKLY A VERY NICE MILK RUN. WHICH
IS ALWAYS WELCOMED.
  OUR H-HOUR WAS 02:45 AND WAS I, SLEEPY, AS USUAL.
IT WAS A VERY NICE WEATHER FOR A MISSION.
  OUR CREW FLEW COMPLETE WITH THE EX-
CEPTION OF OUR CO-PILOT, LT. B.W. HYDE, WAS REPLACED
BY 2ND LT. LIZAK, A ONE OF THE NEW CREWS I
BELIEVE JUST OVER FROM THE STATES.
  TAKE OFF WAS AT 06:00 AND WE WERE
SUPPOSED TO FORM WITH OUR GROUP. OUR SQD
HAD SEVEN SHIPS AND WE WERE TO BE THE
LAST BOX, OUR SHIP "SPORT" WAS TO FLY #4
POSITION. OUR BOX WAS LAST TO TAKE OFF
AND OUR GROUP WAS GONE WHEN WE REACHED
OUR MEETING POINT. WE PROCEDED ON OUR
WAY TO CATCH THEM, OUR C.O. CAPT.SMITH
WAS LEADING OUR SQD. FOR SOME REASON
WE FAILED TO SEE OUR GROUP & LATER
ON WE FOUND WE HAD PASSED THEM. THIS
IS DUE TO US TAKING A SHORT CUT, & IN
DOING SO WE PASSED THEM.

Mission No 28 June 25 1944

Our target today was the combination marshallin[g] yards SOB bases, and oil & storage tanks, at Sete France. It was strickly [strictly] a very nice milk run. Which is always welcomed.

Our H-Hour was 02:45 and I, sleepy, as usual. It was a very nice weather for a mission.

Our crew 810 flew complete with the exception of our co-pilot, LT B. W.Hyde, was replaced by <u>2nd</u> Lt. Lizek, one of the new crew I believe just out from the states.

Take off was at 06:00 and we were supposed to form with our group. Our sqd had seven ships up & we were to be the last box, our ship, "Sport" was to fly No 4 position. Our box was last to take off and our group was gone when we reached our meeting point. We proceeded on our way to catch them, our C.O. Capt Seith was leading our sqd. For some reason we failed to see our group & later on we found we had passed them. This was due to us taking a short cut, & in doing so we passed them.

(2)

We were at about 14,000 ft and on oxygen, when we passed almost directly over Rome. It was a very impressive sight and we had the glasses in the waist, so I had a very good look at it. I could pick out very large buildings and it did not seem to be damaged at all.

Outside of seeing Rome the trip was uneventful, altho' as we came to the French coast we began to think of the possiblities of fighter attacks, as we thought our escort was with the group.

Just before target time the escort showed up altho it proved unnecessary because no fighters were sighted, perhaps due to our escort.

Our bomb run was quiet, without flak, though there was a very little of in the distance. Our target was hit directly, althou I only got to see the smoke. They say it was really in flames.

Just as we turned off the target

(2)

We were at about 14,000 ft and on oxygen, when we passed almost directly over Rome. It was a very impressive sight and we had the glasses [binoculars] in the waists [the main body of the plane; fusclage]. So I had a very good look at it. I could pick out very large buildings and it did not seem to be damaged at all.

Outside of seeing Rome the trip was uneventful. Altho as we came to the French coast we began to think of the possibilities of fighter attacks as we thought our escort was with the group.

Just before target time the escort showed up altho it proved unnecessary because no fighters were sighted, probably due to our escort.

Our bomb run was quiet without flak. Though there was a very little in the distance. Our target was hit directly, althou I only got to see the smoke. They say it was really in flames.

Just as we turned off the target

(8) MISSION NO 78.

WE SAW THE REST OF OUR GROUP MAKE ITS RUN. SO ALL TOLD IT WAS A GRAND JOB OF BOMBING. ALTHO THE TARGET WAS COVERED WITH SMOKE BY A GROUP AHEAD OF US.

WE RETURNED TO OUR FIELD AHEAD OF OUR GROUP. IT WAS A VERY QUIET RETURN RUN.

OUR THE LANDING TIME 13:30. ENTIRE TRIPE 7½ HOURS. A LITTLE LONG, BUT ALL AN EASY WELCOME ONE.

OUR PILOT 1ST 2ND LT. E.R. PROMBERGER MADE 1ST LT TODAY. ALSO OUR BOMBDIER 2ND LT. H. GUERRINA MADE 1ST LT.

NONE OF OUR SHIPS OR THE GROUPS SHIPS WERE DAMAGED TODAY. THATS SOMETHING WE WOULD LIKE TO BE ABLE TO SAY EVERY DAY OF EVERY MISSION.

(3) Mission No 28.

We saw the rest of our group make its run. So all toll [told] it was a grand job of bombing. Altho the target was covered with smoke by a group ahead of us.

We returned to our field ahead of our group. It was a very quiet return run.

Our landing time, 13:30, entire trips 7 ½ hours. A little long, althou an easy welcome one.

Our 1st pilot 2nd Lt. E. R. Promberger made 1st Lt. today. Also our bombdier 2nd Lt. [illegible] Guerrina made 1st Lt.

None of our ships or the groups ships were damaged today. Thats something we would like to be able to say every day & every mission.

My Father and My Uncles

MISSON #29#30   JUNE 26 1944
"LOBAU"
OUR TARGET TODAY WAS THE OIL REFINERIES
SOUTHEAST OF VIENNA AUSTRIA.
I GOT UP AT 03:30 HOUR THIS MORNING.
OUR CREW 810 FLEW COMPLETE WITH THE
EXCEPTION OF THE CO-PILOT. 2ND LT. LIZAK REPLACED
LT. B.W. KIDD.
OUR TAKE OFF WAS AT 06:40 AND IT WAS
VERY NICE WEATHER.
EVERYTHING WENT FINE UP UNTIL TARGET
TIME. WE WERE WITH OUR OWN GROUP, 483 &
IT WAS THE LAST GROUP IN THE ENTIRE AIR
FORCE. OUR SQD WAS NEXT TO THE LAST SQD
TO CROSS THE TARGET. OUR SHIP WAS NO 4 IN
THE NO 2 BOX.
WE DROPPED 20 - 250 LB. G.P. THE OTHER
WAIST GUNNER & MYSELF HAD "CHAFF" TO
THROW OUT TODAY. SO WE DID NOT GET TO
SEE THE MAIN BARRAGE OF FLAK AS WE
PASSED OVER THE TARGET. I COULD SEE A
BIT BENEATH OUR PLANES. F
THERE WERE ABOUT 80 E/A FIGHTERS
REPORTED BUT THEY DID NOT BOTHER

Mission #29 & 30   June 26 1944

Our target today was the "Lobau" oil refineries southeast of Vienna Austria.

Has a 03:30 H-hour this morning.

Our crew 810 was complete with the exception of the co-pilot. 2nd Lt Lizak replaced Lt B. W. Hyde.

Our take off was at 06:40 and it was very nice weather.

Everything went fine up until target time. We were with our own group, 483 & it was the last group in the entire air force. Our sqd was next to the last sqd to cross the target. Our ship was No 4 in the No 3 box.

We dropped 20 – 250 lb. "G." "P." The other waist gunner & myself had "chaff" to throw out today. So we did not get to see the main barrage of flak as we passed over the target. I could see a bit beneath our planes.

There were about 6 or 9 fighters reported but they did not bother

(2)

our box or sqd as far as I know. Our fighter escort was right on the ball.

The tail gunner & myself saw a vapor trail high overhead & assumed it a fighter but he was just fooling around.

On the bomb run I saw some chutes far below which came from a B-17 which was reported going down far ahead of us. A bit further on I spotted two more chutes. We do not know for sure if all of the boys got out, as it was not a "red tail".

I saw our box's bombs hit in a very concreated area & bright flashes were very visable. There were three targets in close about the same area. There were huge clouds of black smoke at all three targets.

We flew a path which was to take us between two areas heavyly guraded with we received a lot of flak bo. it was cross wise to our line of fl... ...after leaving tar...

Jim Hodge

(2)

our box or sqd as far as I know. Our fighter escort was right on the ball.

The tail gunner & myself saw a vapor trail high overhead & assumed it a fighter but he was just fooling around.

On the bomb run I saw 4 or 5 chutes far below which came from a B-17 which was reported going down far ahead of us. A bit farther on I spotted two more chutes. We do not know for sure if all of the boys got out, as it was not a "redtail".[25]

I saw our box'es [sic] bombs hit in a very concreater [? concentrated] area & bright flashes were very visible. There were three targets in about the same area, huge clouds of black smoke at all three targets.

We flew a path which was to take us between two areas heavily guarded [illegible: ? until] we received a lot of flak but it was cross wise to our line of flight. I saw all of it after leaving target

---

[25] Redtail may refer to the identity of my father's group, but the reference is unclear.

and it seemed to spread for several miles to either side of us. To our ourselves we only remained in flak alley for a fairly short time. It's a good thing we flew crosswise to the flak area.

I felt the concussion of one explosion beneath our right wing. Much to my surprise there was no hole there, thank goodness. When we landed we found our left evelator with a large hole in it. It had to be replaced. No other holes received.

Pilot feathered no 4 over target. He discovered it was running away, but not due to en flak. At a lower alt. he brought it back in.

On "after bombs away" I saw a ship going down back at five o'clock. It was far behind & below + just appr to be a huge ball of flame. I don't know what group it was from.

After leaving area of target we had a uneventful return ride with only a few flak bursts off our

(2) [3]

and it seemed to spread for miles to either side of us. Do [due] to our course we only remained in flak alley a fairly short time. It's a good thing we flew crosswise to the flak area.

I felt the concussion of one explosion beneath our right wing. Much to my surprise there was no hole there, thank goodness.

When we landed we found our left elevator with a large hole in it. It had to be replaced. No other holes received.

Pilot feathered No 4 over target. He discovered it was running away, but not due to flak. At a lower alt[itude] he brought it back in.

After "bombs away" I saw a ship going down back at five oclock. It was far behind & below & just appeared to be a huge ball of flame. I don't know what group it was from.

After leaving area of target we had a [sic] uneventful return ride, with only a few flak bursts off our

(-) Mission #29 +30

...ings but way out of range (I'm glad.) Landing time was 13:30. It was 6 hrs and 50 mins.

~~Fles a Vienna Target~~

T/65- Town of Vienna itself is our roughest target as far as flak goes but we were out of range of their guns today. Had we have gone over the city itself it would have really been rough.

~~7/5~~ (We flew in our own ship, 143, today. The best ship ~~he~~ anywhere.)

(4) Mission 29 & 30

wings but way out of range (I'm glad.)

Landing time was 13:30. It was 6 hours and 50 mins.

The town of Vienna itself is our roughest target as far as flak goes but we were out of range of their guns today. Had we have gone over the city itself it would have really been rought [sic].

(We flew in our own ship, 143, today. The best ship anywhere.)

MISSION NO 31   JUNE 27, 1944

OUR TARGET TODAY WAS ORIGINALLY BRIEFED AS
WAS TO BE THE MARSHALLING YARDS AT THE
TWIN CITIES OF BUDAPEST, HUNGARY. IT SO
TURNED OUT THAT WE FINALLY BOMBED THE
MARSHALLING YARDS AT BROD YUGOSLAVIA, A
TARGET WE HAD BOMBED ON OUR SECOND
MISSION, APRIL 13, 1944.

OUR CREW 810 FLEW COMPLETE WITH THE
EXCEPTION OF OUR CO-PILOT. LT. B. W. HYDE. WAS
REPLACED BY 2ND LT. KUTVICK. LT. BOULDIN - S-2 OFFICER FLEW WITH US.

WE HAD A 03:30 H.HOUR THIS MORNING. OUR TAKE
OFF WAS AT 06:40 AND WE FLEW CAPT. BENTLY'S
SHIP 576. WE FLEW NO.4 BOX NO.1 POSITION. OUR
SQUADRET THE OUTFIT.
EVERYTHING WENT FINE FOR THE TRIP
TO THE TARGET WITH THE EXCEPTION OF A CAL 50
ROUND OF AMMO, WHICH WAS CHARGED OUT OF
THE SHIP AHEAD. IT STRUCK & SPLINTERED
THE PILOTS WINDSHIELD, IT DID NOT BREAK
THE INSIDE PANE.

SOON AFTER TAKE OFF OUR CO. CAPT. SETT-
HAD TO TURN BACK DUE TO PLANE TROUBLE. HE
WAS FLYING "PATHFINDER". CAPT. BENETLY

Jim Hodge

Mission No 31 June 7, 1944

Our target today as originally briefed was to be the marshalling yards at the twin cities of Budapest, Hungary. It so turned out that we finally bombed the marshalling yards at Brod Yugoslavia, a target we had bombed on our second mission, April 13, 1944.

Our crew 810 flew complete with the exception of our co-pilot Lt B. W. Hyde was replaced by 2nd Lt Kutnick. Lt Bouldin , J-2 ? [S-2] officer flew with us.

Had a 03:20 H-Hour this morning. Our takeoff was at 06:40 and we flew Capt. Bentley's ship 526. We flew No 4 box in No 1 position. Our sqd let [led] the outfit.

Everything went fine for the trip to the target with the exception of a cal 50 round of ammo, which was charged out of the ship ahead. It struck & splintered the pilot's windshield. It did not break the inside pane.

Soon after take off our C.O. Capt. Smith had to turn back due to plane trouble. He was flying pathfinder. Capt. Bendtly

(2)

MOVED UP TO REPLACE HIM ONLY HE DID NOT HAVE A PATHFINDER SHIP. OUR SQD WAS LEADING THE GROUP BEHIND US.

WE ARRIVED AT THE I.P. ONLY TO FIND THE WEATHER VERY OVERCAST. AT TIMES OUR WINGSHIPS WERE HARDLY VISIBLE. IT WAS FINALLY DECIDED NOT TO BOMB BUDAPEST. AFTER MUCH FLYING AROUND WE FINALLY TOOK OFF FOR BROD. WE SIGHTED A VERY SMALL AMOUNT OF FLAK AT BUDAPEST. DURNING THIS TIME 2ND. LT. OWENS BECAME SEPARATED FROM THE GROUP HE BOMBED THE ORGINAL TARGET WITH ANOTHER OUTFIT WHICH HAD A PATHFINDER. AFTER BOMBS AWAY THEY BECAME LOST AGAIN. JUST ABOUT THIS TIME THE JERRYS WERE MIXIN WITH OUR 38's. AT ONE TIME A P.38 & ME-110 WERE SEEN COMING OUT OF ONE OF THE MANY CLOUDS FLYING FORMATION. AS SOON AS THEY RECONGIZED EACH OTHER THE REALLY MIXED IT UP. LT. OWENS CREW REPORTED ME-109's ME 110 & 210'S THERE WERE

Jim Hodge

(2)

moved up to replace him only he did not leave a pathfinder ship. Our sqd was leading the group behind us.

We arrived at the I.P. only to find the weather overcast. At times our winfships were hardly visible. It was finally decided not to bomb Budepest. After much flying around we finally took off for Brod. We sighted a very small amount of flak at Budepest.

Durning [During] this time 2nd Lt Owens became separated from the group. He bombed the original target with another outfit which had a pathfinder. After bombs away they became lost again. Just about this time the Jerrys were mixing with our 384s. At one time a P. 38 & ME-110 were seen coming out of one of the many clouds. Flying formation. As soon as they recognized each other they really mixed it up. Lt. Owens crew reported ME-109-ME 110 & 210's there were about twenty in all toll [sic]. At various

[A page seems to be missing in the original.]

MISSION NO's 32633   July 2, 1944

OUR TARGET TODAY WAS THE OIL REFINERYS ABOUT 30 MILES EAST OF BUDAPEST HUNGARY IT WAS A VERY WELCOME MILK RUN.

OUR CREW 810 FLEW WITH THREE EXCEPTIONS 2ND. LT. LUKAS FLEW AS CO-PILOT, 1 ST LT. GEORGE SWEAR FLEW AS BOMBADIER & T/SGT. B. FLETHE OUR POSITION WAS NO. 4 SHIP IN NO 4 BOX. OUR GROUP WAS THE LAST ONE ACROSS OVER THE TARGET.

TAKE OFF WAS AT 07:30 HOURS. WE HAD A 03:45 H-HOUR. WE CARRIED 12-500 LB. G.P.S. THINGS WENT FINE AND WE FORMED INTO POSITION AND WENT TO ALTITUDE OUR TARGET TIME WAS ABOUT 11:06.

ON THE BOMB RUN THERE WAS REPORTED WHAT APPEARED AS TWO SHIPS ON FIRE AND GOING. IT WAS SOME DISTANCE OFF AND THE ONLY REPORT OF CHUTES WAS

Mission No's 32 & 33 July 2, 1944

Our target today was the oil refinerys [sic] about 30 miles east of Budapest Hungary. It was a very welcome milk run.

Our crew 810 flew with three exceptions. 2nd Lt Luvass flew as co-pilot, 1st Lt George Swear flaw as bombdier & T/Sgt B. Fletcher.

Our position was No 4 ship in No 4 box. Our group was the last one to cross over the target.

Take off was at 07:30 hours. We had a 03:45 H-Hour. We carried 12-500 lb. G.P.'s. Things went fine and we formed into position. And went to altitude our target time was about 11:00. On the bomb run there was reported what appeared as two ships on fire and going {down]. It was some distance off and the only report of chutes was 1. We do not know whose ship or ships they belonged to.

The sky was over cast & under cast, as briefed. As we came down the bomb run we were suprised to find no flak. Although we were breifed as such, as long as we stayed on course. We were just a few minutes late in bombs away and a large cloud, of which there were many about, completly covered the target. All of our bombs went away fine but right now we do not know for sure if the target was. Our bombdier reported seeing a refinery & storage tanks a little after we dropped our bombs. This may have been our target, if so, then we missed because of early dropping. Yet, it may have been another refinery. Had our target been clear it would have been a great job, because there was no flak to bother us.

(2)

not know whose ships they belonged to.

The sky was overcast and under cast, as briefed. As we came down the bomb run we were surprised to find no flak. Although we were breifed [sic] as such, as long as we stayed on course.

We were just a few minutes late in bombs away and a large cloud, of which there were many about, completely covered the target. All of our bombs went away fine, but right now we do not know for sure if the target [? was]. Our bombdier reported seeing a refinery & storage tanks a little after we dropped our bombs. This may have been our target, if so, then we missed because of early dropping. Yet, it may have been another refinery. Had our target been clear it would have been a great job, because there was no flak to bother us.

(3)

MISSIONS NO. 32030   July 2, 1944

AFTER BOMBS AWAY WE PROCEEDED
HOME WITHOUT MISHAP. THANK GOODNESS.
THERE WERE NO ENEMY FIGHTER SEEN ON
TODAYS MISSION.
  IT WAS A NICE MILK RUN AND I ONLY
SAW ABOUT SEVEN FLAK BURSTS DURING
THE TRIP.
  OUR TARGED COULD NOT BE SEEN EVEN
AFTER LEAVING IT, DUE TO THE CLOUDS.
WE COULD NOT DISQUNISH THE DAMAGE
IN FLICKENED
  OUR LANDING TIME WAS 13:35 AND IT WAS
A GOOD LANDING

(3)

After bombs away we proceeded home with out mishap. Thank goodness. There were no enemy fighter seen on todays [sic] mission.

It was a nice milk run and I only saw about seen flak bursts during the trip.

Our targed [target] could not be seen even after leaving it, due to the clouds. We could not disguinish [distinguish] the damage inflickened [inflicted].

Our landing time was 13:35 and it was a good landing.

MISSION NO 34   JULY 5, 1944

OUR TARGET TODAY WAS THE MARSHALLING YARDS AT MONPELLIER FRANCE. JUST OFF THE COAST. IT WAS A LONG OVER WATER FLIGHT OF 1286 MILES AND A FAIRLY EASY ONE, EXCEPT IT WAS VERY TIRESOME.

H-HOUR WAS 05:45, THE KIND WE LIKE. OUR CREW 810 FLEW COMPLETE EXCEPT FOR LT. KOLBE REPLACED LT. HYDE AS CO-PILOT. WE CHANGED OUR POSITIONS AROUND A BIT TODAY. I RODE THE BALL TURRETT, A VERY CRAMPED RIDE. TO WAS TO. GEORGE TOOK MY SPOT AT R. WAIST. JOHN & LT. SCOTT CHANGED POSITIONS. WE FLEW SHIP 429 "OUR BABY."

TAKE OFF WAS AT 08:30 AND WE FLEW NO 4 POSITION NO 2 BOX OF OUR GROUP. OUR ENTIRE WING BOMBED MONPELLIER AND THE ENTIRE 15 A.F. BOMBED THE AREA AROUND THAT SECTION OF THE COUNTRY.

I GOT IN THE TURRETT A LITTLE EARLY AND BRUSHED UP A BIT ON IT'S OPERATION, AS IT HAD BEEN SOMETIME SINCE I HAD RIDDEN IN ONE. THIS WAS MY FIRST MISSION IN THE BALL. THINGS WENT FINE EXCEPT I WAS VERY

Mission No 34   July 5, 1944

Our target today was the marshalling yards at Monpellier France. Just off the coast. It was a long over water flight of 1286 miles, and a fairly easy one, except it was very tiresome.

H-hour was 05:45, the kind we like. Our crew 810 flew complete except for Lt. Kolbe replaced Lt. Hyde as co-pilot. We changed our positions around a bit today. I rode the ball turret, a very cramped ride it was to [sic]. George took my spot at r. waist. John & Lt. Scott changed positions. We flew ship 429 "Our Baby."

Take off was at 08:30 and we flew No 4 position No 2 box of our group. Our entire wing bombed Monpellier and the entire 15 A.F. bombed the area around that section of the country.

I got into the turret a little early and brushed up a bit on its operation, as it had been some time since I had ridden in one. This was my first mission in the ball.

Things went fine except I was very

(2)

CRAMPED AND I COULD NOT FIND THE HEATA RESTATE TO TURN UP MY HEATED SUITE. GORGE HAD SET IN ON 15 VOLTS ON THE GROUND AND THAT WAS FINE TILL WE REACHED ALTITUDE. THEN I REALLY GOT COLD. THE ONLY HANDLE I COULD FIND BENEATH THE SEAT WAS THE OXYGEN AUTO MIX KNOB. I MISTOOK IT FOR THE REASTAT AND I THOUGHT "T.U.P. ALL I WAS DOING WAS TURNING MY AUTO MIX OFF & ON. IF IT HAD NOT BEEN FOR THE GROUND SETTING OF 15 VOLTS I REALLY WOULD HAVE BEEN A COLD ONE FOR SURE.

WE FLEW OVER CORSICA AND A FEW OTHER ISLANDS. AS WE NEARED THE SHORE WE COULD SEE TOULON AND IT WAS COVERED WITH SMOKE FROM THE GROUPS OVER HEAD.

WE TURNED ONTO OUR LAND FALL AND DOWN THE RUR. GEORGE REPORTED A SHIP IN THE DISTANCE HAD EXPLODED BUT I DID NOT SEE IT. THERE WAS A LOT OF FLAK OVER OUR TARGET BUT IT WAS AIMED AT ANOTHER GROUP COMING OVER AT A DIFFERENT HEADING. A LITTLE OF IT CAME FAIRLY CLOSE BUT I DONT BELIEVE ANY OF OUR SHIPS WERE HIT. I COULD EASILY VERY EASY HAVE BEEN A TOUGH TIME OVER

(2)

cramped and I could not find the heat restat [? Rheostat] to turn up my heated suite. Gorge [George] had set in on 15 volts on the ground and that was fine till we reached altitude. Then I really got cold. The only handle I could find beneath the seat was the oxygen auto mix knob. I mistook it for the reastat and I turned it up. All I was doing was turning my auto mix off & on. If it had not been for the ground setting of 15 volts I really would have been a cold one for sure.

We flew over "Corsica" and a few other islands. As we neared the shore we could see "Toulon" and it was covered with smoke from the groups over head.

We turned onto our land fall and down the Rur. George reported a ship in the distance had exploded but I did not see it. There was a lot of flak over our target but it was aimed at another group coming over at a different heading. A little of it came fairly close but I don't believe any of our ships were hit. I could very easy have been a tough time over

(2) MISSION No 34 July 8/1944

...HE TARGET AND THEY CONCENTRATED THEIR
...IRE ON US. I HAD A VERY VERY GOOD VIEW
...F THE TARGET. THE GROUPS AHEAD OF
...S REALLY PASTED IT AND THERE WERE
...REAT CLOUDS OF SMOKE OVER IT. THERE WERE
...REAT FLASHES WHICH WERE THE BOMBS
...ITTING AND GREATER ONES WHICH WERE
RESULTS OF HITS ON OIL CARS. OUR
GROUP'S BOMBS STRUCK A LITTLE SHORT
OF THE TARGET AND A LITTLE LEFT. THEY
STRUNG out IN A LINE SO A FEW OF THEM
DID HIT THE YARDS. ALL OF THEM WERE
IN THE AREA

PILOT REPORTED A COUPLE OF RED FLAK
BURSTS IN THE DISTANCE AS YET I HAVE NOT
SEEN ANY.

WE STAYED ON COURSE AND TURNED
AWAY FROM THE FLAK AND WERE SOON
OVER THE WATER AGAIN.

THERE WAS NOTHING EVENTFUL ON THE
RETURN RIDE JUST BEFORE WE REACHED
GORSCIA I GOT OUT OF THE BALL. I WAS
PRACTICALLY A BALL MY SELF BY NO...

(3) Mission No 34 July 5, 1944

the target had they constrated [concentrated] their fire on us. I had a very good view of the target. The groups ahead of us really pasted it and there were great clouds of smoke over it. There were great flashes which were the bombs hitting and greater ones which were results of hits on oil cars. Our group's bombs struck a little short of the target and a little left. They strung out in a line so a few of them [did] hit the yards. All of them were in the area.

Pilot reported a couple of red flack [sic] bursts in the distance. As yet I have not seen any.

We stayed on course and turned away from the flak and were soon over the water again.

There was nothing eventful on the return ride. Just before we reached [Corsica] I got out of the ball. I was practically a ball myself by now.

(4)

We saw over a hundred vessels in a harbor near Rome. Got a good look at Rome. It is a huge city. Would sure like to go there.

We landed here at 17:00 which gave us over eight hours on this mission. It would be all right with all of us if we could get milk runs with a little luck for the rest of our missions

(4)

We saw over a hundred vessels in a harbor near Rome. Got a good look at Rome. It is a huge city. Would sure like to go there.

We landed here at 17:00 which gave us over eights [sic] hours on this mission.

It would be all right with all of us if we could get milk runs with a little luck for the rest of our missions.

MISSION NO: 36@36   JULY 8,1944

TODAY OUR TARGET WAS AN AIRFIELD A VERY SHORT DISTANCE FROM VIENNA, AUSTRIA. HAD A FAIRLY EARLY H-HOUR AND I'V FORGOTTEN OUR T.O. & E.T.A. TIME.

OUR CREW 810 FLEW COMPLETE WITH THE EXCEPTION OF 2ND LT. REETS SHAW IN PLACE OF LT. HYDE AS CO-PILOT. ALSO A PHOTO MAN WENT ALONG.

THINGS WENT ALONG ALLRIGHT UNTIL WE HIT THE I.P. ON THE BOMB RUN THERE WAS A TERRIFIC AMOUNT OF FLAK PUT UP AT US. ONE OF THE BOY'S SAW TWO 17's FROM ANOTHER GROUP. ONE BLEW UP & THE OTHER WENT DOWN WITHOUT BLOWING UP IN THE AIR.

I WAS THROWING OUT TIN FOIL ON THE BOMB RUN AND THE FLAK WAS SO HEAVY & THICK THAT IT WAS BREAKING DIRECTLY BENEATH US. I SPILLED MORE "CHAFF" IN THE SHIP THAN I DID

Jim Hodge

Mission No's 36 [35] & 36 July 8, 1944

Today our target was an airfield a very short distance from Vienna, Austria.

Had a fairly early H-Hour and I'v [sic] forgotten our R.O. and E.T.A. time.

Our crew 810 flew complete with the exception of 2nd Lt [? Bret] Shaw in place of Lt. Hyde as co-pilot. Also a photo man went along.

Things went along all right until we hit the I.P. on the bomb run. There was a terrific amount of flak put up at us. One of the boy's [sic] saw two 17's from another group. One blew up & the other went down without blowing up in the air.

I was throwing out tin foil on the bomb run and the flak was so heavy & thick that it was breaking directly beneath us. I spilled more "chaff" in the ship than I did

My Father and My Uncles

(2)

out of it. Each time I attempted to throw it out a burst would scare the heck out of me. We could hear the bombdiers screaming over the inphone for the pilot to turn out of the way of the flak. But it was almost impossible to turn out of it, because it was all around us. The navigator said he had his hands over his eyes and on one ~~~~ look outside he saw one burst right in front of him. In fact there was a lot of it everywhere. The bombs went away fine but we could not tell the results due to the krsurs ahead of us all the smoke pots around the target. No one looks at the target much because there was to much flak close by to think of. In the waist it sounded

(2)

out of it. Each time I attempted to throw it out a burst would scare the "heck" out of me. We could hear the bombdier screaming over the inphone for

the pilot to turn out of the way of the flak. But it was almost impossible to turn out of it, because it was all around us. The navigator said he had his hands over his eyes and on one look outside he saw one burst right in front of him. On fact there was a lot of it everywhere.

The bombs went away fine but we could not tell the results due to the groups ahead of us and the smoke pot's around the targets. No one looks at the target uch because there was to [sic] much flak close by to think of. In the waist it sounded

(2)

MISSION NO'S 35 & 36 JULY 8, 1944

LIKE A HUGE HAILSTONES WERE STRIKING "SPOT"
OUR SHIP (143) WE FINALLY MEET THE
FLAK AREA, AFTER WHAT SEEMED A
LONG TIME.

AS SOON AS BOMBS AWAY WE STARTED
TO RALLY RIGHT AND I WAS SUPPOSE
TO TAKE PICTURES OF THE TARGET. THE
FLAK WAS STILL THERE BUT NOT SO
MUCH OF IT. I TOOK ABOUT 4 OR 5 PICTURES
AND WAS READY FOR THE NEXT, WHEN
ALL HECK BROKE LOOSE AGAIN. WELL,
I GAVE UP THE JOB OF PHOTO MAN RIGHT
THEN & TOOK TO THE ARMOR E PLATE I
MADE AND THEN ATTEMPT TO GET A
PICTURE, BUT IT WAS STILL BURSTING
RIGHT OUTSIDE SO I JUST LAID VERY
LOW.

NONE OF OUR BOYS WERE HIT BUT
ALL THE SHIPS WERE AND 4 OF THE

(3)

Mission No's 35 & 36 July 8, 1944

like a huge hailstones were striking our ship "Sport" (143) We final[y] left the flak area, after what seemed a long time.

As soon as bombs away we started to rally right and I was supposed to take pictures of the target. The flak was still there but not so much of it. I took about 4 or 5 pictures and was ready for the next, when all heck broke loose again Well I gave up the job of photoman right then & took to the armor & plate. I made another attempt to get a picture but it was stiss [still] bursting right outside so I just laid very low.

None of our boys were hit but all the ship were and 4 of the

I had to go to the service sqd. Our wing spars were cut and holes were in both wings. Big sized ones. Our Co. had a shell pass completely thru his R. wing and lucky for them it did not explode. It went thru the tank, and gas' really flew. It was a miracle that the shell was a dud.

We all landed safely and were glad to do so.

I understand a waist gunner was killed in 815 sqd, & the other W.G. had his arm & leg broken from 20 m.m.

It was a costly mission in more ways than one. I just hope we do not have to go back again.

(4)

7 had to go to the service sqd [for] wing [? Spare] were out. And holes were in both wings. Big sized ones. Our C.O. had a shell pass completely thru his R wing and lucky for them it did not explode. It went thru the tank, and gas reall[y] flew. It was a mircial [miracle] that the shell was a dud.

We all landed safely and were glad to do so.

I understand a waist gunner was killed in 815 sqd, & the other W.G. had his arm & leg broken from 20 m.m.

It was a costly mission in more ways than one. I just hope we do not have to go back again.

MISSION No. 37   July 15, 1944

TODAY OUR TARGET WAS THE OIL REFINERY A SHORT DISTANCE FROM PLOESTI, ROUMANIA. OUR SQD. REALLY SUFFERED HEAVY LOSSES TODAY.

OUR K-NOOR WAS 3 OCLOCK, WITH TAKE OFF AT 5 OCLOCK.

WE WERE FLYING NO 4 POSITION IN NO 3 BOX. THERE WERE TWO WINGS GOING OVER THE SAME TARGET.

OUR CREW DID FLEW COMPLETE WITH THE EXCEPTION OF LT LETHERMAN FOR LT. HYDE SOON AFTER TAKE OF NO 6 SHIP HAD TO TURN BACK AND LATER ON OVER YUGOSLAVIA NO 7 SHIP HAD TO TURN BACK.

OUR TARGET TIME WAS ABOUT 10:05. WE WERE COMING DOWN THE BOMB RUN AND I WAS THROWING OUT THE CHAFF. I COULD COULD NOT SEE THE FLAK OUT THE SIDE BUT COULD SEE A LITTLE BELOW US. IT WAS OVER CAST AND THEY ALSO HAD SMOKE POTS BURNING. WE COULD FEEL AND HEAR THE FLAK BURST AND JUST AS THE BOMBS WENT AWAY WE HIT A LOT OF PROP WASH AND I REALLY THOUGHT

Mission No's 37, July 15, 1944

Today our target was the oil refineries a short distance from Polesta [Ploiesti], Romania. Our sqd. really suffered heavy losses today.

Our H-Hour was 3 oclock, with take off at 6 o'clock.

We were flying No 4 position in No 3 box. There were two Wings going over the same target.

Our crew 810 flew complete with the exception of Lt. Letherman for Lt. Hyde.

Soon after take off No 6 ship had to turn back and later on over Yugoslavia No 7 ship had to turn back.

Our target time was about 10:05. We were coming down the bomb run and I was throwing out the chaff. I could not see the flak out the side but could could [duplicate word in original] not see a little below us. It was overcast and they also had smoke pots burning. We could feel and hear the flak burst and just as the bombs went away we hit a lot of prop wash and I really thought

My Father and My Uncles

our turn had come. I'd had scares before when over the target, and when we were hit, but this time I really thought we were going down. It happened so quick it bounced me around on the floor and my gun bounced up to the ceiling. By the time I got myself off the floor I saw the radio man looking out the B-bay to see if it were clear to jump. The B.T. man had his door open looking out. We all had the same feeling that we were going down. After we dropped we went down in a bit of a glide, so that made us sure we were hit.

We soon got back in formation and found we were hit in the No Two oil tank. Oil was spraying out but not too badly so the pilot did not feather it. Our No 1 ship had No 1 feathered right after bombs away and a very few minutes later he feathered No 3. He was hit in the gas tank and I could see the gas spraying out. No 2 ship had No 2 feathered. I'm not sure but I think No 3 had No 3 feathered. Our No 2 was not feathered yet and No 5 had all four running. Our Sqd fell far behind because of the

(2)

our turn had come. I've had scares before when over the target, and when we were hit, but this time I really thought we were going down. It happened so quick it bounced me around on the floor and my gun bounced up to the ceiling. By the time I got myself off the floor I saw the radio man looking out the b. bay to see if it were clear to jump. The b.t. man had his door open looking out. We all had the same feeling that we were going down. After we dropped we went down in a bit of a glide so that made us sure we were hit.

We soon got back in formation and found we were hit in the No two oil tank. Oil was spraying out but not to[o] badly so the pilot did not feather it. Our No 1 ship had No 1 feathered right after bombs away and a very few minutes later he feathered No 2. He was hit in the gas tank and I could see the gas spraying out. No 2 ship had No 2 feathered. I'm not sure but I think No 3 had No 3 feathered. Our No 2 was not feathered yet and No 5 had all four running.

Our sqd. fell far behind because of the

My Father and My Uncles

(I) Mission #57 1/8/44.

Lead ship only having two engines running a little ways off the target. The Jerries jumped us. I saw about three of them, and I got in a few shots, but they were all a little out of range. They made a few passes at us and it looked like flak bursting but it was their 20mm. The lead ship called the escort and they drove the Jerries off. It was a little noisy for a few minutes with all those 50's going.

After the fighters left No 1 ship began to throw things over. They were flying the Mickey ship and we do not know why they did not drop the radar ball. We were about four thousand feet and everyone seemed to be doing alright. They threw everything out, and we were well in Yugoslavia, and it was cloudy and we were coming to huge cloud bank. The No 1 ship's No 3 engine was giving out large puffs of black smoke. I guess they knew it would soon go out so they started to bail out. I saw four chutes and they were so close I felt I could pull the cord for them. Capt Habbena the bombadier

Jim Hodge

(3) Mission #37 7/15/44

lead ship only having two engines running. A little ways off the target the Jerries jumped us. I saw about three of them, and I got in a few shots, but they were all a little out of range. They made a few passes at us and it looked like flak bursting but it was their 20 mm. The lead ship called the escort and they drove the Jerries off. It was a little noisy for a few minutes with all those 50's going.

After the fighters left No 1 ship began to throw things over. They were flying the mickey ship and we do not know why they did not drop the [? rav dar] ball. Were [We] were about 7 or 8 thousand feet and everyone seemed to be doing alright. They threw everything out and we were well in Yugoslavia, and it was cloudy and we were coming to a huge cloud bank. The No 1 ship's No 3 engine was giving out large puffs of black smoke. I guess they knew it would soon go out so they started to bail out. I saw 7 or 8 chutes and they were so close I felt I could pull the cord for them. Capt. Harrell the bombdier

(2)

-ant out the nose and I missed him. I could see the slipstream catch him and the jerk they got when the chute opened. One boy had a delayed jump and I was scared to death that his chute would not open. It finally did just before he was out of my sight. Just as we hit the cloud bank the 5th man jumped, but I did not see him. The ship sailed in the cloud and that was the last we saw of them. The 10th man should have gotten out alright. I sure hope he did. At Valwitch's No. 4 (no 2 ship) was feathered and we ran most sight of each other in the cloud. When we came out he was not in sight. We found the No. 3 & No. 6 ship and we all stayed together.

After we hit the sea the l. waist gunner saw a ship ditch and we circled to find them but no luck. The other two ships came on in and they all thought we had gone down.

We had to come in because our No. 2 was ____feathered and we were low on gas.

(4)

went out the nose and I missed him. I could see the slip stream catch them and the jerk they got when the chute opened. One boy had a delayed jump and I was scared to death that his shoot would not open. It finally did just before he was out of my sight. Just as we hit the cloud bank the 9th man jumped, but I did not see him. The ships went in the cloud and that is the last we saw of them. The 10nth man should have gotten out alright. I sure hope he did. Lt. Valvitch's (No 2 sip) No 2 engine was feathered and we all lost sight of each other in the cloud. When we came out, he was not in sight. We found the No 3 and No 5 ship and we all stayed together.

After we hit the sea the 1. waist gunner saw a ship ditch and we circled to find them but no luck. The other two ships came on in and they all thought we had gone down.

We had to come in because our No 2 was now feathered and we were low on gas.

(5) MISSION #37 7/18/44

WE FINALLY LANDED AS THE LAST SHIP TO LAND.

WE LOST ONE SHIP FOR SURE. TODAY WE HEARD THAT A B-24 CREW WAS PICKED UP ON THE SEA. SO WE DO NOT KNOW WHAT HAPPENED TO LT. KAUMAN.

HOPE WE DO NOT HAVE ANY MORE DAYS LIKE THAT.

7/10/ THE 6 BOYS WHO BAILED OUT 32 DAYS AGO OVER YUGO GOT BACK HERE TODAY. THEY SAID THEY REALLY HAD SOME EXPERIENCE.

(5) Mission #37 7/15/44

We finally landed as the last ship to land.

We lost one ship for sure today 7/15. We heard that B-24 crew was picked up in the sea. So we do not know what happened to Lt. Kalvach.

Hope we do not have any more days like that.

7/15/ The 5 boys who bailed out 32 days ago over Yugo got back hear [here] today. They said they reall[y] had some experience.

JULY 21, 44

MISSIONS NO'S 38 & 39

OUR TARGET TODAY WAS BRUX OIL REFINERIES IN CZECHOSLOVAKIA.

OUR CREW WAS SPLIT UP FOR THE MISSION. THREE OF US FLEW WITH 1ST LT. HYDE. THE OTHER THREE ENLISTED MEN FLEW WITH 1ST LT. LETHERMAN.

BILL, PETE & JIMMY FLEW IN 631, THE REST OF US IN 819.

JIMMY WAS KILLED OVER THE TARGET BY INTENSE FLAK. BILL SAID HE WAS STRUCK IN THE HEAD & LEG & ALL OVER. HE DIED ABOUT FIVE MINUTES AFTER GETTING HIT. IT MUST HAVE HORRIBLE I HOPE AND PRAY IT DOES NOT HAPPEN AGAIN. IT SURE IS AWFULL STRANGE AND DIFFERENT WITHOUT JIMMY. THERE WILL BE FEW JOKES & LAUGHS AROUND OUT

Missions No's 38 & 39   July 21, 1944

Our target today was "Brux" oil refineries in Cechoslovakia.

Our crew was split up for the mission. Three of us flew with 1st Lt. Hyde. The other three enlisted men flew with 1st Lt. Letherman.

Bill, Pete & Jimmy flew in 631, the rest of us in 919.

Jimmy was killed over the target by intense flak. Bill said he was struck in the head & leg & all over. He died about five minutes after getting hit. It must have horrible. I hope and pray it does not happen again. It sure is awfull [sic] strange and different without Jimmy. There will be few jokes & <u>laughs around out</u> [our] tent from now on.

Mission No 40   July 24, 1944

Our target today was the ball bearing works near   in N. Itah.

Our crew, we do not have Timmy with us Harry, we flew with 1st Lt. Long + Scott. S/Sgt Snyder flew Tail & S/Sgt Perkins flew Bank.

It was a rather long jingle counter but proved to be a milk run. We would all like the rest of them just like it.

We all landed safely and got our bombs away in good order. We had 12 clusters loaded with insinder. I think the target was weak 16 T. We flew 788 today, a good ship. The 301st was directly beneath us and I think our bombs scared them, and I don't blame them.

Mission No 40   July 24, 1944

Our target today was the ball bearing works near _____ in N. Italy.

Our crew, we do not have Jimmy with us now, we flew with 1st Lt Long & Scott. S/Sgt Synder flw tail & S/SSGD Perkins flew ball.

It was a rather long jingle counter but proved to b [sic] a milk run. We would all like the rest of them just like it.

We all landed safely and got our bomb away in good order. We had 12 clusters loaded with insinderies [incendiaries]. I think the target was well hit.

We flew 288 today, a good ship. The 301st was directly beneath us and I think our bombs scared them, and I don't blame them. ~

MISSION 130 4/ JULY 27, 1944

OUR TARGET FOR TODAY WAS THE AIRCRAFT PLANT & STEEL WORK AT BUDAPEST HUNGRY.

OUR CREW FLEW WITH OTHER OUTFITS. THE FLAK WAS VERY HEAVY OVER THE TARGET. T/SGT. OLDEN WAS HIT BY FLAK IN THE STOMACH AND PASSED AWAY THE 28TH.

WE FLEW INTO BRON'S FLAK GUNS ON THE COAST, BUT LUCKY FOR US WE DID NOT GET HIT. OUR SHIP 352 SIG TO SHIP HAD ABOUT 3 HOLES.

THERE WAS LOTS OF BOMB'S DROPED AND THE TARGET WAS DESTROYED.

OUR BOMBS HUNG UP AND WE REALLY HAD A TIME. IT TOOK ABOUT AN HOUR TO GET THE DOORS CLOSED.

TAKE OFF TIME 06:30, LANDING TIME 12:10 TARGET TIME 09:45.

Jim Hodge

Mission No 41   July 27, 1944

Our target for today was the air craft plant & steel work at Budapest Hungary.

Our crew flew with other officers. The flak was very heavy over the target. T/sgt Olden was hit by flak in the stomach and passed away the 28th.

We flew into Bron's flak guns on the coast but lucky for us we did not get hit. Our ship 352 816th ship had about 3 holes.

There was lots of bomb's [sic] droped [sic] and the target was destroyed.

Our bombs hung up and we really had a time. It took about an hour to get the doors closed.

Take off time 06:30, landing time 12:10 target time 09:45.

MISSION NO 42.   AUG, 3, 1944

TODAY OUR TARGET WAS GERMANY. JUST EAST OF LAKE _____ WHICH IS THE LINE BETWEEN GERMANY & SWISS.

OUR SHIP was 526 TODAY. LT BROMBERGER OUR PILOT. ALT 26,000 FT WITH UNDER CAST.

WE BOMBED _____ AND THE RESULTS WERE _____.

WE WERE BRIEFED ON 68 GUNS ON BOMB RUN, BUT WE WERE LUCKY DUE TO OUR ALT & A LOT OF SHIPS FAR BELOW US. WE HAD A VERY VERY EFECTIVE P-51 COVER & DID NOT SEE JERRY.

~~WE WERE SUPPOSED TO GE~~

WE ARRIVED SAFELY BACK HOME AFT A 7 HR & 55" MIN FLIGHT.

Mission No 42   August 3, 1944

Today our target was _____ Germany. Just east of Lake _____ which is the line between Germany and Swiss.

Our ship was 526 today. Lt Promberger our pilot, Alt 28,000 ft with under cast.

We bombed _____ and the results were.

We were briefed on 68 guns on bomb run, but we were lucky die to our last Alt & a lot of ships far below us. We had a very very effective P-51 cover & did not see Jerry.

~~We were supposed to go~~

We arrived safely back home after a 8 hr & 55 min flight.

4/19/44

MISSION NO 44

Lt. WHITED WAS PILOT & WE FLEW #52, AT 26,000 FT.

OUR TARGET WAS PLOESTIE, ROMANIA.

WE WERE LEADING OUR SQD, AND NO 2 TURBO AMPLIFIER FAILED. WE COULD NOT KEEP UP WITH GROUP SO WE DROPPED OUR BOMBS ABOUT 15 MINUTES FROM THE TARGET. WE HAD 2 P-51s FOR A FEW MINUTES AS ESCORT HOME, BUT CAME BACK MOST OF THE WAY ALONE.

THE WEATHER WAS VERY HEAVY & BAD & WE HAD A HARD TIME HOLDING ALTITUDE. LANDED SAFELY ABOUT

Jim Hodge

Mission No 44   8/19/44

Lt. Whited was pilot & we flew 257, at 26,000 ft.

Our target was Polesti [Ploiesti], Romania.

We were leading our sqd., and No 2 turbo amplifier failed. We could not keep up with group so we dropped our bombs about 15 minutes from the target. We had 2 – P-51's for a few minutes as escort home, but came back most of the way alone.

The weather was very heavy & bad & we had a hard time holding altitude. Landed safely about

(?)

30 MINUTES AHEAD OF GROUP.
WE WERE NOT SURE OF RECEIVING CREDIT
BUT DID, FOR OUR BOMB'S BLEW
UP A HIGHWAY. WHICH WAS NEEDED
BY THE ENEMY.

(2)

30 minutes ahead of group.

We were not sure of receiving credit but did, for our bomb's [sic] blew up a highway which was needed by the enemy.

2/22/44

Mission: No 5/5"#46

Our target was synthetic oil & cocking plants at Ödertal Germany. Altitude was 23,500 ft. and our ship was 405". It's first mission.

We hit the target and as well as we could tell, for it was cloudy, but it looked good. We flew a path between our targets flak & that of Brecknum flak. Thank goodness we were not hit. As far as I know one ship in the group was hit. They came in on two engines and without the ball. As far as I know no one was hurt. Thank goodness.

8/22/44

Mission's No 45 & 46

Our target was synthetic oil and cocking [coking] plant at "Odertal" Germany. Altitude was 27,500 ft. and our ship was 405. It's [sic] first mission.

We hit the target as well as we could tell, for it was cloudy, but it looked good.

We flew a path between our targets flak & that of Breckammer's flak. Thank goodness we were not hit. As far as I know one ship in the group was hot. They came in on two engines and without the ball. As far as I know no one was hurt. Thank goodness.

AUGUST 23,

MISSION NO'S 47 & 48

OUR TARGET TODAY WAS THE AIRCRAFT PLANT AT WIENNER NEUDORF, ABOUT TEN MILES SOUTH OF VIENNA AUSTRIA.

OUR PILOT, LT. WHITED FLEW 018 PATHFINDER, NAMED "MARGE", OUR CO's WIFE'S NAME.

OUR ALT. WAS 26,500 FT. WE HAD A FINE ESCORT OF 51's & 38's

THERE WAS LOT'S OF FLAK AND WE TURNED AWAY FROM IT A SHORT DISTANCE FROM IT. AS WE RALLIED RIGHT WE ENCOUNTERED FLAK AT 3 O'CLOCK, BUT IT WAS A LITTLE DISTANCE OFF OUR WING AND I WAS VERY THANKFUL FOR IT. THERE WERE FOUR TURN BACKS IN THE GROUP. ALL PLANS RETURNED

August 23, [1944]

Mission No's 47 & 48

Our target today was the aircraft plant at Wienner Neudorf, about ten miles south of Vienna Austria.

Our pilot, Lt. Whited flew 018 pathfinder, named "Marge", our CO's wife's name.

Our Alt. was 26,500 ft. We had a fine escort of 51's & 38's. There was lot's [sic] of flak and, we turned away from it a short distance from it. As we rallied right we encountered flak at 3 o'clock. But it was a little distance off our wing and I was very thankful for it. There were four turn[ed] back in the group. All plans [planes] returned

(+)
SAFELY. A COUPLE SHIPS GOT A VERY FEW HOLES, BUT WE WERE LUCKY & I THANKFUL.

(2)

safely. A couple ships got a few holes, but we were lucky and I [was] thankful.

LAST ONE 9/25/44

MISSIONS NO 49 & 50

TODAY WAS MY LAST MISSIONS AND AM I HAPPY.

OUR PILOT WAR 1ST LT KLICKO, AND HE, 1ST LT GUERRINA & MYSELF ALL FINISHED TODAY.

OUR TARGET WAS THE AIRFIELD AT LISEN (NE BRNO) AND AIRCRAFT FACTORY.

OUR ALT. WAS 24,000 FEE & I FLEW TAIL GUN POSITION.

THERE WAS ONLY ONE BURST OF FLAK OVER THE TARGET. IT WAS A SWELL MILK RUN SO TO SPEAK, BUT WE SWEAT THEM ALL OUT. ESPICALLY TODAY & ESPICMANY ME.

WE LANDED WITH NOT TO MUCH GAS LEFT, BUT IT WAS A GOOD MISSION.

JOHN & PETE WILL FINISH IN A COUPLE

9/25/44

LAST ONE

Mission 49 & 50 9/25/44

Today was my last mission's [sic] and am I happy.

Our pilot was 1st Lt Klicko, and [unreadable], 1st Lt Guerrina & myself all finished today.

Our target today was the airfield at Lisen (nr Brno) and aircraft factory.

Our Alt. was 24,000 fee[t] & I flew tail gun position.

There was only one burst of flak over the target. It was a swell milk run so to speak, but we sweat them all out. Especially today & especially me.

We landed with not to[o] much gas left, but it was a good mission. John & Pete will finish in a couple

of DAVE.
I'm very THANKFUL TO FINISH SAFE
I JUST WISH ALL THE BOYS COULD
HAVE DONE THE SAME.

"FINITO"

(2)

of days.

I an thankful to finish safe. I just wish all the boys could have done the same.

~

"Finito"

My Father and My Uncles

Jim Hodge

Appendix B

At the time of the Colonel's death in 1997, Jim Irvine wrote the following in honor of Colonel Hank Mucci. It describes the significance of Jim's pack mule unit becoming Army Rangers and Mucci's leadership in making this happen.

Mucci's Rangers

By Army Ranger Jim Irvine
May 1, 1997

A stocky Lieutenant Colonel sporting a neat Clark Gable moustache and a sun-bleached fatigue hat stepped briskly onto the hillside platform. He stared down at the 800 dejected, disgruntled men of the 98th Pack Mule Artillery. The men of the Pack stared back. They stood in the boiling New Guinea sun. The backs of their faded green fatigues were wet with sweat. As the Colonel stepped forward, a low murmur rose from the restless ranks. He did not blink an eye, even as he sensed the general attitude of the men, voiced just audibly by one of the sweating soldiers, "What the hell have I gotten myself into now."

This was Papua New Guinea in June, 1944. It was an awesome assignment, to convert this disillusioned mob into a crack Ranger Battalion within ninety days. Their morale was lower than a lizard's larynx. They had followed the wide butts of a thousand Army mules up and down the steaming foothills of the Owen Stanley Mountains for a year and a half. They had caught only fleeting glimpses of the enemy at 10,000 feet in the sky. Lack of purpose, loss of pride and sheer boredom had all but destroyed this once elite unit.

The Pack had initially been chosen as the biggest, toughest men in the U.S. Army.

They boasted that they could out-walk the infantry by one mile an hour. The 98th Pack had scaled Pike's Peak as a unit just a few months earlier.

Good raw material for a Ranger battalion? Maybe, ... Just maybe.

The silver oak leaves glistened and moved with the sturdy shoulders as the Colonel in the white fatigue hat began to talk. One by one the mule skinners began to listen. This was the beginning. One by one faces began to change. First a glimmer of hope, next a grin, then here and there a chuckle. In minutes they were shouting and cheering. The transformation was a tribute to the charisma of the man in the white fatigue hat. We now had a leader! We had a purpose!

From that day forward these big guys were no longer dejected mule packers; in spirit they were already Rangers. In ninety days, their bodies and minds would follow.

They would become, as Hank said, "The best damned soldiers in the world."

Those were your words, Hank, spoken with tears streaming down your cheeks, on the day they promoted you out. You have been promoted again. With tears in our eyes we now say, lead on Hank, your Rangers will still follow you anywhere.

From the men of the 6th Ranger Battalion to their beloved commanding officer, Col. Henry A. Mucci, at his passing on April 27, 1997.

Acknowledgements

I am grateful that, through in-person and written interviews with these six men, I was able to capture the majority of the information in this history. They are all gone now. I pray that for our families, and I hope future generations of our families, this record will serve them well, as well as be of interest to other readers.

A thank you to the following individuals whose recollections helped make this history possible.

John Cook
Hilda Dixon
Linda Dixon
Cameron Hodge
Harry Hodge
Jenny Hodge
Sue Hodge
Jim Irvine II
Jim Irvine III
Marge Irvine
Don Morris

Elsie Morris
Liz Marx
Norton Most
Y. John Nickolas
Shawn Petipren
Delton Polk
Don Reed
Jean Reed
Maggie Reed
George Stovall

And I consulted the following sources:

The Detroit News

John Costello: "*The Pacific War*"

H.Q. 483rd Bomb Group

Indiana Board of Tourism

National Geographic World Atlas; Washington D.C.

National Military Personnel Records; St. Louis, Mo.

U.S. News and World Report; New York, N.Y.

Westover Air Field; Westover, MA.

Sally Brodie, Cromaine Library, Hartland, MI

The author also must give a hearty thank you to this book's editor, Donna Nakagiri, and my publisher, Red Recliner Books of DMS Onge Publishing, LLC. Like many writers the author has counted heavily on his publisher to put this history in presentable condition.

About the Author

Jim Hodge is a veteran who served in the Demilitarized Zone on the Korean peninsula in 1966 as a Sergeant in the U.S. Army, 2nd Infantry Division. He later served as an assistant instructor at the Army's Officer Candidate School at Fort Benning, Georgia.

He graduated from Wayne State University in Detroit where he met his beautiful wife Sue.

Jim is also the author of the novel, *When Troubles Rain*. The home front scenes of his novel are set in the environs of Stoughton, Wisconsin. The military scenes in *When Troubles Rain* are set in the austere Korean peninsula where Jim learned to appreciate a desperately poor people's struggle to remain free.

The Hodges live northwest of Detroit. They have two adult children and three amazing grandchildren. Jim is a member of the Military Writers Society of America.

Also by Jim Hodge:

When Troubles Rain: A Novel
10th Anniversary Edition
with two new special notes by the author

With deftly drawn characters, Jim Hodge illuminates the heritage, culture and beliefs of the Norwegian-American Berg family as they work their way through life during difficult times.

Through love, strong family ties and a strong community, the Berg family faces war, tragic loss, and mysterious threats to their way of life. Meeting each trouble that arises with grace, faith, and a good dose of stoicism, the Berg family makes their way through life.

This unassuming historical novel is powerful and serious, yet touched with humor. It recognizes the horrors of war, yet stresses the family's dedication to God and country.

This is a book to renew the values of patriotism, hard work, family, sacrifice, and gratitude.

Available through your favorite bookseller, online at *Amazon.com* and *BarnesAndNoble.com*.

My Father and My Uncles

Jim Hodge

About the Publisher

We hope you enjoyed this wonderful military family history, *My Father and My Uncles: One Family's Call to Service in World War II*, by Jim Hodge.

We are a traditional publisher and accept a limited number of manuscripts. We have previously published a novel by Jim Hodge, *When Troubles Rain*. We hope he continues to write and that we may continue to publish his works, as well as works by other equally wonderful American authors.

Our books are available through your favorite bookseller, online at *Amazon.com* and *BarnesAndNoble.com*.

*DMS Onge Publishing, LLC, publishes
fiction and nonfiction works under a number of imprints,
including this imprint, Red Recliner Books,
as well as greeting cards and other printed products.*

My Father and My Uncles

www.ingramcontent.com/pod-product-compliance
Lightning Source LLC
Chambersburg PA
CBHW070507240426
43673CB00024B/465/J